FED UP of being fed up
AT WORK?

A must-have resource for professionals
who wake up on Monday morning wishing
its was Friday afternoon!

DION JOHNSON

Edited by Mildred Talabi

Fed up of being fed up at work?
A must-have resource for those who wake up
on Monday morning wishing it was
Friday afternoon!

By Dion Johnson

Published by Purple Circle Publishing
Suite 18, Bradley House, Aspinden Road
London SE16 2DL
Copyright © Dion Johnson 2013

Cover Design: Richard Horsford
Book Design & Typesetting: Richard Horsford

A CIP catalogue record is available for this book from the British Library.

ISBN 978-0-9567946-0-4
Printed and bound by CPI Group (UK) Ltd, Croydon, CRO 4YY

FED UP of being fed up
AT WORK?

Purple Circle Publishing

Dedication

This book is dedicated to my best friend J.C.
It is because of you that I know the truth of who I am.
It is because of you that I dare to believe that I can
make a difference in the world So this book is a firstfruits
offering to you from me; an expression of all I am
because you love me.

With love and thanks from the
bottom of my heart.

DJ

Acknowledgments

Thanks to my daughter Bianca for putting up with
me throughout the years of "pregnancy" with this book and
to the mega-talented Mildred Talabi whose excellent
writing and editing skills helped me to birth it!

And to Grandma Hazel who allowed me to turn her spare
room into my office cum labour room. I am extremely grateful to
you grandma for your love, patience, practical help
and encouragement.

And I want to take this opportunity to say a special
thank you to the people God chose to raise and train me
so I could live this life and make a difference. Clementina & Keith
Johnson, my extraordinary parents; Bishop John and Co-Pastor Penny
Francis my spiritual parents who pray diligently for me, and Pastor
Enid Stewart, the most profound teacher I have ever met.

Wayne Malcolm, Sue Knight, Tim Gallwey,
Les Brown and David Shosanya
extraordinary mentors and teachers.

Denise Johnson-Carr, my little sister
you are my true friend through thick and thin

To all of you I say Thank you, I am standing tall because
you allowed me to climb up on your shoulders.

I couldn't have done it without you.

Love you all so much!

*"Today we come across an
individual who behaves like an automaton, who does
not know or understand himself and the only person that he
knows is the person that he is supposed to be; whose meaningless
chatter has replaced communicative speech, whose dull
despair has taken the place of genuine pain."*

Erich Fromm

"Here is Edmund Bear, coming downstairs now;
bump, bump, bump, on the back of his head, behind
Christopher Robin. It is, as far as he knows, the only way of
coming downstairs, but sometimes he feels that there really
is another way, if only he could stop bumping for
a moment and think about it."

Winnie the Pooh

Contents

Foreword

This is a wonderfully inspiring book which will take you on a real journey of transformation: from having Monday-morning blues which last till Friday, to looking forward to your working week with a genuine sense of excitement, enjoyment and enthusiasm!

I first met Dion Johnson at a Positive Psychology Masterclass which I co-facilitate in Bristol. As soon as she walked into the room I knew that there was something special about her. Dion is a woman with a clear mission, but not in an overpowering or self-important way that you sometimes find in successful and highly motivated business people. Dion radiates the vitality, warmth and confidence of a leader who is authentic, self-aware and humble – rare qualities indeed. I soon realised that despite our different backgrounds, we share many experiences and interests, not least our professional roots, our personal quest to rediscover the passion for what we do every day, and our desire to help other people unlock their potential in work which they find fulfilling, meaningful and fun.

Think about those words again –fulfilling, meaningful and fun. Can you honestly apply them to the job you do? And can you imagine enjoying your work so much that you call it play? Let's face it, work can be hard, and organisations can be tough places at times - it would be unrealistic to expect otherwise. And feeling that you're stuck in a job rut, not knowing what to do and lacking the energy and enthusiasm to get out of it can make them seem even tougher. But don't underestimate the importance of feeling good about your job and the organisation your work in – after all, you spend roughly a third of your time there. In Dion's words, you need to make sure that your work works for you.

If you've read this far, then there's something about being fed-up of being fed-up at work that rings true for you. Deep-down you know things need to change. This book is the catalyst you need. It provides the essential motivation and momentum to start you on that journey, as well as the inspiration, support and encouragement to sustain you along the way. Using simple, practical exercises, helpful hints and tips and real-life insights, this book will enable you to identify what you want from your job, discover how your personal qualities can help achieve the work that works for you, and prepare you for your unique journey towards the life you want to live.

Dion Johnson is living proof that discovering work which is exhilarating, challenging and motivating can change your life. Whether you're cautious and quiet or bold and ballsy, this book is for you. Read it and be inspired to pack your bags and wave goodbye once and for all to those Monday-morning blues and give a warm and wholehearted welcome to work you love.

Bridget Grenville-Cleave, MSc MAPP
WorkMad Ltd
Making Business Human

Introduction

This book is aimed at people who are fed up of being fed up at work. Notice I said "fed up of being fed up" and not just fed up! If it were just for people who are simply fed up, almost everyone would need this book because there is strong evidence to suggest that a massive proportion of the global workforce, if the truth be told, just cannot stand their job. In preparation for this book, I stopped 1,000 people on their way to work in the morning and asked them: "How do you feel about going to work today?"

The results were fascinating; this is some of what they said:

- *"What's the option below hate?!"*
- *"How do you think I feel? It's cold and I haven't finished sleeping yet!"*
- *"Let's put it this way, I'm already thinking about home time!"*
- *"No I can't say that on camera, my boss might see it!"*
- *"Dislike the idea... a lot! I've only been there a couple of months so that's really bad isn't it?"*
- *"I don't like to think about it 'cos I've got no choice really."*
- *"Who likes going to work? No one! I'm no different."*
- *"I think most people hate the idea of going to work, but there is no choice."*
- *"Gotta pay the bills!"*
- *"Erm, honestly? I don't hate going to work, I just dislike it – intensely!*

A staggering 61% of my random sample were less than thrilled at the prospect of doing their job that day. This is by no means peculiar to my research; in fact, if you go into any pub on a Friday evening you are bound to overhear the moans and groans of people who want to "get off their chest" just how difficult their week at work has been and how they are dreading Monday morning. That's why the term 'Thank God It's Friday' (TGIF) exists! When I tell people about the topic of my book, invariably they let out a little chuckle and make some kind of comment about how many people (usually themselves included), need a book like this. What is interesting about the conversations I had around this topic is that people genuinely feel they have no choice other than to just put up with their job even though they are unfulfilled, unhappy and just plain sick of it.

I completely disagree. It is just not true that you have to stick with a job that's not working for you as though you are some kind of chained prisoner, but yet there are millions of individuals who settle for just that, becoming a slave to their work. There are millions who get up every morning feeling miserable about the idea of going to their job and who spend the day longing to get out of there. Literally, for much of the workforce, going to work is like doing time! Have you ever walked into a public service only to be greeted by a sour-faced receptionist who is far from courteous? Or perhaps you have sought professional support or advice from someone who made you feel like you were the biggest inconvenience on the planet? I think most of us can answer yes to these questions because fed up workers are everywhere! More to the point, fed up workers to a very large degree stay in the place where they are most fed up, making their lives and everybody else's lives a misery.

So this book is not for everyone. It is for those who know that they are fed up at work and are ready to make a change. If this is you, then you are in the right place. I am delighted to be able to walk alongside you on this journey; I am inviting you to embark on a process, one that aims to not just make work bearable for you, but to make work meaningful, stimulating and more fulfilling – or as I like to say, to make work work for you.

That meaningful, fulfilling work life doesn't just land on your lap and I have yet to find a magic wand that you simply wave and "WALLAH!!" you wake up in your dream work experience. Rather, you must decide what you want and set about deliberately creating it in your work life. I believe that truly satisfying work is work that has a strong relationship with who you are and what you want to achieve with your life and not just a necessary evil to be endured so that the bills get paid.

This book is about taking a good look at yourself in order to work out what you really want from work. It is about understanding yourself because being fed up at work is a symptom and a clue that something is wrong. Just as with a physical symptom, like frequent headaches for example, you have a choice: you can just keep taking painkillers and treating each headache as it comes or you can begin to search for the cause of the headaches. Both approaches aim to rid you of the pain but the first requires that you just accept that headaches are a part of your life while the latter, I would argue though more labour intensive, will give you the information you need to live free from the ailment.

My aim is not to tell you how to change your job (although you may decide to do so as a result of reading and working through the chapters); instead it is about equipping and empowering you to take charge of your work life experience. The information and exercises within the book are designed to provoke you to think about your current situation and to help you identify the way out. You will uncover fabulous things about yourself and perhaps some things you may have forgotten, and you will identify flaws in your character and behaviour that you need to address and change if you truly want to "cure" your ailing work life.

In the last five years of working with people who are fed up at work, I have seen almost miraculous results and breakthroughs in people's working lives as they embark on the journey of aligning their work life with their truest self. Just like Jane who found the courage to tell her husband that she no longer wanted to be his PA, or Sarah who finally took the leap to turn her hobby of floral design into a business, or Tom who realised that he didn't have to give up his beloved city job because of difficult team relations, I guarantee that the processes in this book can help you if you are ready for change.

Pack your 'bag'!

As you work through the book, you will be guided to ask yourself questions and search for the answers. You will look for clues and evidence that will shed light on things that are important about you and to you. All of this information will be invaluable on your journey from the place of being fed up to the place of becoming fulfilled at work.

It is really important that you find a way to store the information you gather. You will find plenty of space in the book to make notes and document your thoughts and discoveries, but rather like packing a bag for a trip, I suggest that you also use a journal or a file on your computer if you need to and carry this 'bag' with you on this journey.

It is also important that you work at your own pace – you might read the book in one sitting or you may decide to read it chapter by chapter every day, giving yourself time in between to explore and record in more depth how it relates to your life at work. The key thing is that you do the thinking and search out the clues and answers for your 'bag'. Do not be put off by how simple the exercises and questions appear, they are important and they have the power to enable you to transform your experience at work, and in turn, the rest of your life.

Are you ready…? Let's go!

Preface

MY STORY

The long awaited Friday evening had finally arrived. I sat at my desk and glanced at the clock – it was 7pm and everyone had already gone home. I switched off my computer for the last time and looked at the boxes with my personal belongings inside, wondering how I was going to get it all into my car. As I looked around the empty office a strange feeling came over me and I knew deep down in my soul that I would never be coming back this way again – EVER!

That was 17th December 2004, a day that is now permanently etched in my memory as one of the most significant milestones of my life and the start of what for me has been an amazing adventure of self-discovery. It was the day I took a huge risk and made the boldest step ever in pursuit of a fulfilling work life.

That year I had a wake up call and the dawning realisation that my life was supposed to be moving. I was busy doing lots of things but all of a sudden it became crystal clear that I was busy going nowhere. I sensed a great journey ahead of me and a still small voice inside beckoned me to COME! The problem was that I was stuck and had no clue whether the path I perceived in my heart was real; furthermore, I had no idea where it would all lead. Just about all I knew was that I simply had to find out.

It seemed crazy to some at the time because prior to this I had been a real career girl. A healthcare professional with a pretty impressive track record, I held a fairly senior government officer position and earned a good salary. I was also a property investor with a nice little portfolio and I drove a nice, brand new car, lived in a nice home and things looked good for me, or so it seemed. I knew in my heart that there was more for me. Everyone thought I was losing the plot when

I announced that I was leaving. At work some people were blatantly ticked off, especially when I told them that I didn't have a job lined up and that I was going to take some time out to find myself. Some people openly expressed their annoyance and asked, "How come you get to do that? I can't afford to just swan off whenever I feel like it." Others just rolled their eyes and patted me on the shoulder as if to say, "Oh, you poor thing, you're losing it. The pressure of the job is really getting to you."

That's when I really became conscious of the state that most of us are in at work: almost like robots, programmed to 'do', we get up each day and go to work without thinking, without questioning and without challenging where we are going and why we want to get there. We're unhappy and unfulfilled but do not dare to think about doing anything about it so we just accept it and live with it in an unthinking, unchallenging but very complaining sort of way.

At that point in time, I was glad to be getting away from people like that and made a promise to myself that I would never again fit into that mould. I didn't imagine that just five years later this would be the basis for my first book and that I would be launching my crusade to radically transform the way we think about our jobs.

As I look back in retrospect, the strange thing about it is that even though I was dissatisfied with my life and despite all that was wrong with my "death" at work, I was caught up in a comfort zone. I was hooked on the money and the fact that I always had more month left at the end of my money was evidence that I could not afford to do anything about my situation. I needed this job and so for years I didn't even think of doing anything about the way I was thinking – I was unconsciously settling for less.

Leaving was the hardest thing I have ever done. It felt like I was leaving certainty for uncertainty, jumping out of the frying pan and into the fire. The day after leaving I woke up thinking, "What in God's name have I done?!" But five years later I am still here, still alive, and I've never gone to bed hungry! If I said my particular journey was easy I would be lying. I have learned some valuable life lessons and my life is taking on a beautiful shape and direction. I have a massive vision that now dominates my life: I see a world where we are taught and encouraged to connect with our purpose and potential and to express it in everything we do, including work. I am fully persuaded that we no longer have to "put up and shut up" with a job that is not doing anything for us.

Since 2004, I have been fortunate to meet and work with hundreds of people who had decided to do something about being fed up at work. Not all of them leave their job like I did, but all of them have radically transformed the way they experience work, and their life as a whole, for the better – this stuff really works!

I am writing this book with YOU in mind. It is my way of using what I have learnt personally and professionally over the past five years to reach as many people as possible. However, I know the message contained within these pages is not for everyone because not everyone who is fed up at work is interested in doing something about it. My desire is for every single fed up worker on the planet to know that it doesn't have to be that way – you too can have a fun, fulfilling and meaningful life in and out of work!

Once you finish reading, I would love to hear your story on how this book has impacted your life. You can connect with me via the website www.dionjohnson.com and if you know of friends, family and colleagues who are also fed up at work, do them a favour and pass on this book.

Enjoy the journey and I look forward to hearing from you.

DJ

1

Section 1
UNDERSTANDING YOUR SITUATION AT WORK

This first section of the book is about understanding what it means to be fed up at work and exploring, in particular, what is happening in your own situation. Understanding 'what' and asking yourself 'why?' are crucial starting points in the change process because only then will you be able to identify the specific strategies that will make a real difference to you at work.

Ch. 1
ARE YOU FED UP
AT WORK?

(Identifying the symptoms)

The fact that you are reading this book goes some way to suggesting a couple of things:

That all is not well with you on the work front;

That you are thinking about doing something to change or improve your situation.

If that is the case, then I anticipate that as you read this chapter you will able to identify with some or even all of the symptoms highlighted here. But first, what does it mean to be fed up at work?

Everyone has bad spells at work – times when things seem to be challenging, stressful, boring, unfulfilling or maybe a mixture of all these and more. In fact, I believe you will be hard-pressed to find someone that has never felt this way on the job at one point or another. This does not necessarily mean that there is a problem at work because usually, these times pass as quickly as they come.

Reaching the state of being fed up at work however, is a different thing. The term 'fed up' is an old, 18th century colloquial expression that alludes to being overfull from overeating. The dictionary definition is "to become weary, or sick and tired of someone or something; or to have reached the limit of tolerance or patience with it". It suggests that someone or something is no longer pleasing and the appetite for it has diminished. You may be able to identify with this if you have ever tasted something so good that you ate it over and over again until you find yourself becoming sick of it. Soon, the thing that once tasted so fabulous becomes unpalatable.

Becoming fed up with your favourite dessert, song or shirt is relatively simple to cope with as you can just omit them from your life with little or no real consequence. But when you become fed up with your job, that's a whole different ball game and doing something about it for most people is not as simple as just walking away.

The Symptom Cycle

It can be all too easy to dismiss the signs or symptoms that our work life is crying out for attention. These symptoms are a very real part of the fed up worker's experience and each of them is a catalyst for the other, serving to perpetuate and exaggerate the state of being fed up at work.

As in the case of the chicken and the egg, it is often difficult to be sure which comes first, but what is clear though is that each symptom has the potential to be both the cause and the effect of feeling fed up at work, and when neglected or left untreated, they can be of tremendous negative consequence to the fed up worker in and out of the workplace, producing what I call "the fed up symptom cycle". *(see fig. 1)*.

Fed up Worker

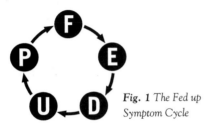

Fig. 1 The Fed up Symptom Cycle

The first obvious symptom of being fed up at work is that you do not want to be there. Many people have the experience of getting up every day to go to a job they would rather not be doing and so find themselves seemingly trapped in the fed up symptom cycle. Below are some other indicators of a fed up worker which you may well recognise in yourself:

🅕 – Forgetting Your 'Why'

"Remember to keep the main thing the main thing"

People who are fed up at work have usually forgotten the reasons they loved the job in the first place. There is an emotional detachment from the elements of the role that made it pleasurable and a lack of connection with the original motivations that made the job an attractive proposition.

I was reminded of this recently when I bumped into Sally, a nurse that taught me when I was a student midwife. Sally had been very kind to me and I admired her a lot; she had taken me under her wings and poured everything she knew into me at that time. Sally was very ambitious and I always got the sense that she was going places. She would often tell me that this role was a stepping stone to lead to her big dreams and personal objectives, which included her vision and plans to impact women's health and develop maternity services in her country of origin.

On our chance encounter, I asked Sally what happened to all her plans and zeal for improving women's services. She just shrugged her shoulders and with an insincere laugh said, "Ahh...too old for that now. I haven't really thought about those things for a long time." I was more than a little taken aback that Sally seemed to have given up on those personal motivations and plans which were such a big part of who she was, and which served as the fuel to her enthusiasm all those years ago. I struggled to work out how someone so driven and focused could find themselves so off track and disengaged from their original purpose. I realised then that it was because Sally had forgotten her reasons for doing the job in the first place and as we spoke, I could sense that she was as sad about it as I was.

E – Energy drain
"The world's number one energy crisis is Monday morning"

Another symptom that people who are fed up at work experience is an increasing lack of energy. This occurs because there is a strong correlation between our emotional state and our levels of energy, and since being fed up at work is an emotional condition, it is no wonder that fed up workers often feel excessively and inappropriately tired during the work day – even after a good night's sleep!
Over the years, clients and friends have told me many amusing stories

about how they create a secret snooze corner somewhere in the building (I have to say, the toilet seems to be the place of choice for this little trick!), or how they have learnt to position props so that they look like they are busy working while they take a much-needed power nap! Fed up workers often experience a constant energy drain throughout the work day and may find themselves yawning frequently, watching the clock, slouching on the desk and dreaming of climbing into bed – only to find that as soon as they leave work there is an almost miraculous revival and a fresh spring in their step!

Others experience a drop in energy levels not just when at work, but even at the thought of work, and some report a real difficulty in "switching off" from work when they leave, or that the energy drain spills outside of work hours and invades their energy levels at home and at social occasions too.

Ⓓ – Dissatisfaction

"Don't just work for the money, that will bring only
limited satisfaction" – **Kathy Ireland**

Staff satisfaction is the most measured variable in staff surveys because not only is it a crucial measure of organisational success, it is also a critical ingredient to high-level enjoyment and engagement at work. Commonly, fed up workers become dissatisfied with various facets of work including pay, promotion, supervision, relationships with co-workers, and fulfillment within the job itself.

According to the dictionary, dissatisfaction is "the state of feeling unfulfilled". It speaks of a failure to meet needs, expectations and desires, therefore to be dissatisfied at work is tantamount to being in an environment where your needs are not being met. Just like any other environment where human needs are consistently unmet, this can have a massive impact on your personal sense of value as well as physical wellness.

Fed up workers with low job satisfaction are most likely to experience emotional burn-out, have reduced self-esteem and raised anxiety and depression levels. Even a modest decrease in job satisfaction can lead to a burn-out of considerable clinical importance. A study carried out by Lancaster University Management School and Manchester Business School in 2005 analysed over 250,000 individuals and found that job satisfaction critically influenced employee health, and that dissatisfaction at work is the cause of significant emotional strain which directly affects the risk of mental health illness. If prolonged, dissatisfaction will affect performance and levels of achievement at work, which leads nicely to the next common symptom experienced by people who are fed up at work.

Ⓤ – Underachievement

"I feel sorry for the person who can't get genuinely excited about his work. Not only will he never be satisfied, but he will never achieve anything worthwhile" – **Walter Chrysler**

Underachievement is the failure to perform appropriately in line with aptitude and ability. Fed up workers often find their levels of achievement decreasing until they are getting less and less done throughout the working day, week and even year.

Whilst this below-average performance may come up as an observation during appraisal, there is also a possibility that it may go unnoticed because fed up workers often do just enough to keep from drawing attention to themselves, in fear of reprimand or even getting the sack. They satisfy the minimum input and outcomes needed to blend in but often though, they are punching way below their weight in terms of performance and are certainly not pushing any performance boundaries or reaching their true potential.

ⓟ – Passionless

"Without work, all life goes rotten. But when work is passionless, life stifles and dies"

Passion can be likened to "fuel" for life, yet a fed up worker often experiences an increasing lack of passion for work and anything associated with it – everything "work" appears to be dull and gloomy. Since passion lubricates the ability to get the job done and makes things smooth and easy, it is a well-accepted fact that most things become much more difficult, taxing and challenging to do without authentic passion. A lack of passion can forge a serious dent in the fed up worker's level of confidence, persistence, drive and motivation to get the job done well and relate to colleagues and customers.

As you were reading about these symptoms, you may well have recognized yourself in some or all of these descriptions. The next chapter will help you to explore where you are on the fed up at work spectrum a little further, and will give you the opportunity to identify some of the issues that need to be dealt with in your unique and particular case.

Ch. 2
SO, WHAT'S REALLY GOING ON WITH YOU AT WORK?

In the first chapter we looked at some of the symptoms associated with being fed up at work, which you may well have identified with in some cases. Although these feelings and experiences are common in the workplace, it is important to understand them in a personal way. As you take the time to look more closely at where you are and what is happening to you at work, you will uncover valuable clues about what might be causing these experiences. Almost invariably, you may find that the causes and reasons for these are different and deeper than what you may have initially thought.

If you want to change and improve your experience of work from the way it is now, getting clear about where you are will not only provide you with a record and a reference point that you can use to look back on as you begin to make real progress in your work life, it will also arm you with information you will need to develop your strategies and plans for changing and improving your experience of work. With this in mind, below are some exercises that will help you take a closer look at what is actually happening and why work is not working for you anymore.

When you are doing these exercises, it is important that you are honest with yourself about your feelings and experiences. I appreciate that this is not always easy since we often get into the habit of "prettying things up" or concealing how we really feel about things at work. We do this perhaps in part so that we don't have to face up to the challenge that comes when you can no longer ignore that it is time to do something about the way you have been feeling, or perhaps because you don't want to rock the boat and make things more difficult than they already are with your colleagues and managers.

I know from my personal and professional experience of work that it can be easier and more 'normal' to take a deep breath, throw your shoulders back and just get on with the job, than to be honest about how things are really affecting you. I want you to make up your mind right now that you will be completely honest with yourself throughout this process. When determining your current position, it is vital that you describe the situation as it is and as objectively as possible. Be realistic; this is a chance for you to call a spade a spade – the more honest you are, the more chance you give yourself of making the right changes to get the work life you really want.

Your responses to these questions will point to relevant and important information about your situation at work, which you will need to begin to formulate an understanding of what you need to address in order to make things better. Ask yourself, 'Why do I?' or 'Why don't I?' 'Where did that start or stop?' 'Do I like this?' 'Why don't I like that?' Remember, the more you dig, the more you are likely to find, so approach these exercises like your favourite TV detective – become inquisitive and curious about sniffing out clues and solving them!

Avoid the temptation to dwell on the negative, rather, be as objective as you can be, taking time to search out the good as well as the bad and the ugly. At this point try not to justify yourself or point the finger of blame. I have resisted the temptation to create one of those predictive diagnostic style tests because I think you are in a much better position than I am to interpret what your answers mean – you are after all the expert in your life. Be mindful of this and remember that the exercises are just triggers to focus your mind and guide your thinking. Make a note of anything that pops into your mind as you do the exercises. The information you glean here is crucial information for the bag as it will shed light on where you are, not necessarily geographically, but emotionally and experientially with your job.

EXERCISE ONE: THE WHEEL OF WORK

This wheel of work has been adapted from the 'Wheel of Life' which is an assessment tool widely used in coaching to help people "locate" themselves. You will see that within the wheel there are spokes or lines that go from the centre point of the circle to the outer rim. Each line represents an aspect of work life that contributes to the overall experience on the job.

Each spoke or line has a numerical scale that represents a score for that particular aspect of your job. The scoring starts at 0 where each line connects with the central point of the circle, to 10, where the line meets the perimeter of the circle.

Here is what you will need to do: Consider each line or aspect of work individually and ask yourself, 'How happy am I about this area of my work? How well am I doing with it?' Discuss the answer and take note of your responses so that you can give yourself a score of 1-10 depending on how happy and fulfilled you are with that particular area.

1 = Very low score and signifies
discontentment and dissatisfaction in this area
10 = Very high score and signifies high levels of
satisfaction and fulfillment in that area.

Mark your score 1-10 at the appropriate point of each line:

Once you have plotted your score for each of these important facets of work life, join the dots. How does your work wheel look? Is it smooth? Can you see areas that need to be worked on in order to make work a more balanced and fulfilling experience?

THE WHEEL OF LIFE

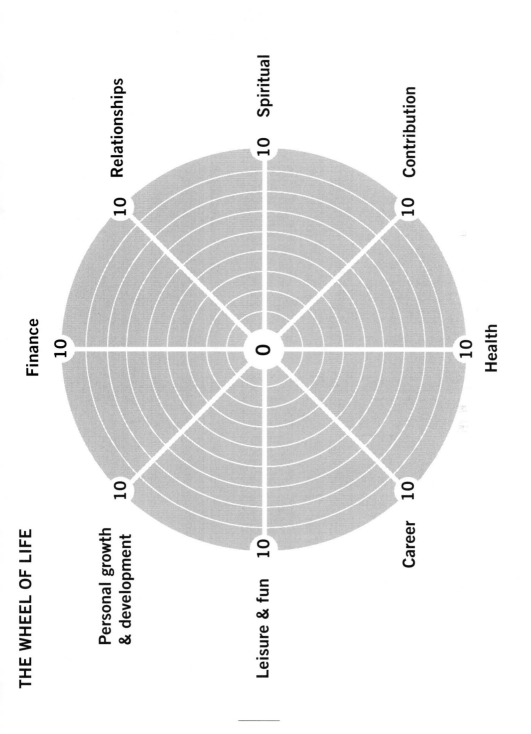

EXERCISE TWO: QUESTIONNAIRE

Read the statement in column one and tick the most appropriate answer relating to how much you agree with it.

	Strongly Agree	Agree	Disagree	Strongly Disagree
1. On my way to work in the morning I am usually looking forward to getting there				
2. I love this line of work				
3. I feel I make a valuable contribution to the success of my department				
4. I feel I make a valuable contribution to the success of the company/organisation				
5. My work day usually goes by very quickly				
6. I enjoy my job very much				
7. If I had the opportunity to do any job I wanted to I would still choose this job				
8. Doing this job is a strategic part of my overall career plan				
9. When it is time to leave this job, I feel confident and very capable of getting the job I choose				
10. I never take time off sick unless I am sick				
11. When I am not at work I talk about my work fondly with family and friends				

At this stage, it is fine if it is not yet clear to you how this information is useful in the process of transforming your work life. Even if you are not sure what you can do to overcome some of the challenges that you have identified, don't worry, you are still on track. This is a process and every step will make a difference to your new destination so just put it in the bag for now and let's move on to the next chapter...

Take it a little further...

Identify the three areas that received the lowest scores and think about what has or is contributing to such poor scores in these areas:

1st Area	Score
Reason for low score	

2nd Area	Score
Reason for low score	

3rd Area	Score
Reason for low score	

Great! You should have identified some really useful information about where you are and what is happening around your experience at work. This next exercise is again designed to get you thinking in a more focused way about what is really going on with you at work.

Ch. 3
ARE YOU IN THE WRONG JOB?

Now that you have had a chance to take a closer look at what you are experiencing at work, how do you feel about your job? There is a growing body of evidence that most people at some point or other question if they are in the right job. While this might be no more than a reaction to a bad spell at work, research has shown that many people (one study suggested one in five) consider that they are in the wrong job. In fact, 41% admitted that they had been in the wrong job at some point in their careers. This means then that a significant number of people are fed up at work simply because they are in the wrong job.

But what makes a job wrong for you? I have identified three main causes for what I call the "wrong job syndrome".

1) Wrong because it never was right

As I mentioned earlier, as part of the research for this book I asked a thousand people on their way to work in the morning how they felt about the idea of going to work that day. Out of the sample, 61% were not enthusiastic about their job and I was surprised at just how many of them were new in their role.

Interestingly, when I asked people to share their answer on video, I met at least 30 people who told me they could not be filmed as they had been in the role for less than two months and did not want to do anything that would jeopardise it – some seemed guilty and almost embarrassed to admit that they were fed up at work so soon after starting.

There are many people who are fed up at work right now because the job they are doing was never the right job for them. They made a mistake but just kept going with it, almost as if to say that once you start a job you are locked in indefinitely and have to stick at it.

2) Right does not mean right forever

I remember when I first qualified as a nurse, I got a job on a neurological medicine ward and I loved it. Everything seemed perfect for about a year then things started to change. Nothing seemed new and exciting

44

any more and the staff that I worked with started to move on and new people came in to join us. There were strategic changes within the unit too so that my experience at work became dramatically different to when I first started – things changed, I changed, my colleagues changed and the unit changed.

I like to call change a universal law because it is inevitable. That means that even if the job starts out right, chances are that it won't continue to be right forever. A wrong job is not necessarily a bad thing, instead it should be thought of as an indication, a sign that your work life needs attention.

3) Poor understanding of what right means for you

The psychology behind the way people select their job is far more complex than we have the time to delve into now. Over the years, I have talked to and worked with hundreds of professionals, asking them why they are doing the job they are doing and I have been astounded by the significant numbers of people who pursued jobs and careers that they considered to be "good jobs" rather than the perhaps more important consideration of what the right job might be for them. What's more, this seems to be a cycle that is set to continue because I regularly have young people say to me, "I just want a good job."

In my attempts to understand what people are calling a "good job", I observed that those jobs generally regarded as good are ones that are culturally considered good, either by the individual's family or peers, or the wider society in which he lives. Often these are professions that require years of training and offer what is widely considered an important service to the community and the world at large, such as doctors, lawyers, teachers and accountants. However, the traditional definition of a good job also includes jobs that command a high level of respect and status, such as chief executives and politicians, with a relatively good salary that is perceived to be able to provide you with an easy, fun and luxury-filled lifestyle.

My take on this is that many people (too many for my liking) are in the wrong job because they are more motivated to find jobs that will impress other people and show them in a good light, or jobs that prove their intelligence or their great value and ability, rather than a job that would be more suited to their truest passions and desires. Of course, this is not true of everyone but I have heard enough about it from numerous clients over the years that I think it is worth a mention here. There is nothing wrong with impressing people, conforming to social value systems, or even earning lots of money and having lots of things; however, it is essential that you begin to look within to see who you really are in order to determine what is good and right for you in terms of work.

A key aim of this book is to help you identify work that is not just good, but one that is right for you. Use the space below to explore your own motives for applying for your current role and keep this as useful information for the bag.

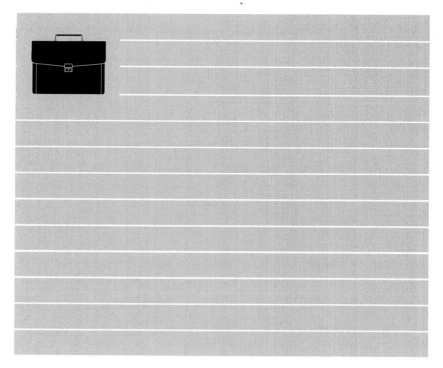

Ch. 4
WHY WE GET
FED UP AT WORK

One of the most important lessons I have ever learnt is the importance of asking questions. I believe that asking questions is one of the most effective ways to begin making anything in life better so if you are fed up at work and want to change that, you must learn to ask yourself probing, searching and challenging questions.

The question 'why' is a good place to start – it offers insight and understanding that is going to shape the road to improvement of your work situation. Asking why is a powerful way to really begin to move from the way things are to the way you would like them to be. Your answers to the question why are valuable as they transport you from the place where you are just feeling and experiencing being fed up at work, to a place of understanding and options where you can now choose to do something about your situation.

It is important to know what is happening but if you want to change your situation you will have to move your thinking from the place of what to the place of why. By asking why, you create the space to begin to take control and to create new possibilities for yourself for new feelings and experiences.

There are three main reasons why people become fed up at work:

1. They are in the wrong job, but don't know where is right
2. They are in the wrong job, and would rather be somewhere else
3. They are in the right job, but have the wrong focus

Reason 1: Wrong job – don't know where's right

This first reason of being in the wrong job with no idea of what the right job would be is rooted in hopelessness.

I had loved nursing for many years but after a while it became just like living in a bad dream. Going to work was such a strain for me as I did not want to be there and the anticipation of it would literally make me feel unwell. However, everything was so chaotic in my life at the time and I had debts to pay off so even though I felt unhappy at work, I felt there was just no alternative. I had no ideas or visions of what I could be doing instead or where I would go and I could not imagine doing anything that would pay me the same wages. I felt like I didn't have any choice so I just stuck at it for many more years.

I come into contact now, on almost a daily basis, with people who are clearly as hopeless about their work situation as I was. These people know that they do not want to do it anymore but they have almost resigned themselves to staying stuck, simply because they do not know what else they would do instead. It is almost as if a silent but powerful little voice goes off in their head saying, "Ah well, that's it then; if you don't know what you want then you'd better stay here…"

Feeling trapped in a job with no sense of hope for the future contradicts the need we all have to grow, increase, multiply and advance. This need is an inherent part of the human design and when it is not acknowledged in the work environment, workers can easily become fed up. When we find ourselves in situations that do not allow us to express this aspect of our being, the result is inevitably harmful – it almost becomes toxic to our system, producing a poisonous effect on our lives which can manifest in symptoms like the ones we identified in Chapter One.

Reason 2: Wrong job – would rather be somewhere else

This second reason why people are fed up at work stems from a state of frustration and intolerance. Just like reason number one, you are in the wrong job but this time you know what you would love to do instead.

Take the popular TV show The X Factor, for example: you will find that many of the contestants (including Leona Lewis, who made history as the first British solo artist to top the American Billboard chart) testify of having had a 'normal' job prior to being on the show. They describe how fed up they were at their job and almost invariably describe sitting at their desk totally disengaged from what they were supposed to be doing, while they yearned for their dream of musical superstardom to come true.

The fed up worker in this category is experiencing some kind of challenge or obstacle in the way of progress to where they want to be, which can be internal or external. We will go into this in more depth later on, but for now it is just important to recognise that wanting to do something but feeling held back and hindered is a disempowering position to find yourself in.

Unconsciously, many in this second category experience an inner conversation about why what they really want to be doing cannot happen. The result of this is that they either fall into blame mode, attributing their failure to progress to an external factor or circumstance, or they begin to suffer from decreasing levels of self-esteem as they perceive that they do not have what it takes to push past the barriers to get to where they really want to be.

Some people who know what they want never go after it, but instead spend time and energy trying to detach themselves from their true desire in order to settle for what they are doing now. This suppression and denial of true expression is difficult to maintain over time without it having a definite impact on the way you feel about what you are doing – this in itself is capable of causing people to feel really fed up at work.

REASON 3: RIGHT JOB – WRONG FOCUS

This third and final reason occurs because of distraction. The fed up worker likes the role, has chosen to be in this role and essentially should be happy at work. However, something or someone is distracting their attention from the elements that made the job great.

My most recent example of this came with a new client who was previously a high-flying executive. He had an exemplary résumé and was well-known in his field for his outstanding financial achievements, but despite this he was fed up at work. After much soul-searching, he left his executive job to pursue his passion for the protection of the environment. He described his new role as "totally the right thing" – he was passionate about the issue, completely committed to making a difference in this area and most of all he loved it. But yet about a year later, he found himself becoming fed up at work again and he couldn't explain why.

Together we discovered that this was absolutely the right role for him but he had become distracted from all the things that he loved about the role and instead became fixated on how he thought other people valued what he was doing. He felt that he had lost his ability to be as impressive as he was when he was a successful executive and this was jeopardising his fulfilment in what was essentially the job of his dreams. This is quite a common experience amongst fed up workers and the challenge here is to refocus on the aspect of the role that made it the right job for you in the first place.

Which category best represents your situation? As we go on, you will gain tools to address this and help you to move onto a more fulfilled work life, or as I like to say, "work that works for you". In the next chapter I want to take the question of why you are fed up a little further.

Ch. 5

GOING DEEPER: THE THREE LEVELS OF WHY

In the last chapter I outlined three common reasons why people get fed up at work. If you are fed up on your job at the moment, then I expect you may have found yourself in one of the three categories. However, these were very general and surface descriptions of what is really taking place to cause you to be fed up at work and if you are to be successful at making work work better for you, then more exploration is required, which is why I want to introduce you to the three levels of why approach.

To explain what this is all about, it is probably better if I start by telling you how I discovered it: When my daughter Bianca was young and I asked her to do something, she would say "Why, mummy?" And when I answered her, she would say "But why, mummy?" And when I answered that, she would again say "Why?" I know some of you can identify with this – sometimes the dialogue was sweet and endearing and other times...well, let's just say it was a tad inconvenient! But the truth is that there is definitely something to be learnt from our young ones in this area, which is what I call "The Three Levels of Why".

You see, every time there was another why, it forced me to look deeper and deeper into the matter until I was able to share greater and greater insight and understanding with my very inquisitive little person. I noticed that the more she asked why, the more links were established between things that seemed totally unconnected at first glance. For example, the answer to the first why when I instructed Bianca to eat her vegetables was "Because I said so!" but by the third why, the answer was "Because I love you!"

Each level of why reveals another level of insight

This is a simple example but one I hope emphasises the point that why takes you below the surface of the matter to a place where you can find gems of revelation and insight that you can put in the bag for your journey to making work work for you. I have come to appreciate the magic of at least three levels of why and I am encouraging you to give it a try because the more you understand why you are fed up at work, the more equipped you become to make the necessary changes. It may be appropriate in your situation to ask why 4 or 5 times but the important thing about this approach is not so much the number of times you ask why, but the number of times you need to ask why to get to the heart of why you are feeling fed up at work.

So the three reasons outlined in the previous chapter are just the first level of why; I'm suggesting that you go deeper: "Why would I give up the fight to achieve my dream job? Why don't I know what I want? Why would I tolerate this when I know it's wrong for me? Why am I unable to get the experience I want from this job?" These are excellent questions and worthy to be asked if you are serious about moving forward.

It's not your boss or the workload, it's YOU!

If you buy into the three levels of why approach, I guarantee that at some stage as you ask why, you will encounter more and more about yourself and the way you think. This is important because contrary to popular belief, the real reason you are fed up at work is not the work or anything about the job, it is to do with what is happening with you.

Your experience of everything you are going through at work, and in the rest of your life for that matter, is shaped by you and in particular, what I call your Primary Experience Regulators (PERs). These are aspects of your being that govern the way you view and interpret everything you come into contact with. These are:

Your values

Values are those ideals that really matter to you, the things you hold as special and important. In relation to work, values are those things that you consider give purpose to the job. It is values that create the strong desire that makes you take action to get or to keep something that enhances you as an individual. During the process of asking why, you will uncover clues about what you most value, and importantly, where your experience at work is misaligned with your individual core values.

Your beliefs

Beliefs, simply put, are thoughts that you are convinced are true and accept as fact; something you are certain about. Beliefs often become so ingrained due to repeated situations which seem to prove their legitimacy, that it can often be erroneously mistaken for absolute truth. Once you believe a thing your decisions become intrinsically affected by what you believe.

Your attitude

Your attitude is a state of mind revealed through your behaviour. It is a reaction or response to your level of like or dislike for a thing, in this case, work. Attitudes are generally positive or negative and are basically a reflection of core values that you live by. It is expressed by evaluating a particular thing with some degree of favour or disfavour, so your attitude will dictate the way you experience that thing.

Your skills & capabilities

Skills are something that you have learned to do and capabilities are your ability to perform. There are five key skills that are generally required of workers in the workplace:

1. Communication
2. Technology/resource management
3. Working with others
4. Improving own learning and performance
5. Problem solving

When you ask why you are fed up at work you may well uncover clues that indicate that you have a key skill deficit that needs attention. It is important to note that this deficit may be actual – where your level of skill really does fall short – or perceived, where you just believe that you are not well-skilled. Whatever the case, evidence suggests that there is a strong correlation between job attractiveness and satisfaction and your ability to actually perform well in your role.

Your behaviours & habits

Your behaviours are your actions or reactions. They can be conscious or unconscious, overt or covert, and voluntary or involuntary. They are usually manifested in relation to your environment. Building on this, habits are routines of behaviour that are repeated regularly. They tend to occur subconsciously and automatically without direct thought. The important thing to recognise about behaviours is that they are an outward manifestation of the internal working of your thoughts, and just like any action, they will act as a catalyst for an effect or a result of some sort. As you ask why you are fed up at work, you may well be presented with yet more clues that point to the fact that it is some behaviour or habit that you are displaying that is contributing to your negative experience at work.

It can all change

Often, it is not always comfortable to face up to the answers that asking why will uncover, however it is absolutely necessary and empowering to do so if you are serious about moving forward. There is no doubt that the risk exists that you will not like some of the things you find out about yourself, but the good thing is that you are now on the way to doing something about it. Keep this fact locked firmly in the front of your mind and cut yourself some slack! None of us are perfect but only some of us, you included, have started on the road to getting serious about doing something about your life so no matter what you are finding out, give yourself a pat on the back for actually taking the time to look and hopefully go on to fix some things.

Regardless of what you are doing and thinking to produce your experience of work, the good news is that you have a choice – you can choose to change or stay the same; you can begin to decide whether your thoughts and behaviours are creating the outcomes you want and if not, you can do something about it. Your values, beliefs, attitude, skills & capabilities and behaviours & habits are all subject to change. Even if you have held them for as long as you can remember, even if you cannot yet imagine life without being the way you are right now, I promise you that you can and you really ought to begin the process of working out what you want to hold on to and what you want to change so that these aspects of your being become conducive to the work life experience that you most desire.

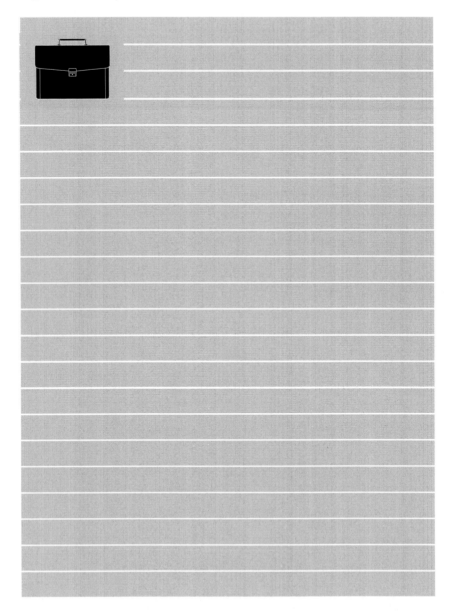

Section 2

UNDERSTANDING WHO YOU ARE AND WHAT YOU WANT FROM YOUR JOB

Recently I was co-facilitating a workshop with a friend where the topic was public speaking. My friend asked the participants to spend a few moments considering their personal vision and aspirations and initially there was some unrest in the room until eventually someone piped up and asked, "Are you talking about our personal vision and aspirations, or our work ones?"

I had heard people say this many times before but yet I still felt sad at hearing it once again and found myself wondering why we so often consider our work life separate from our personal life – after all, are we not the same person? A lot of people think that they have to be somebody else to make it in the workplace, but over the years I have come to understand that when people become committed to finding and developing their true self and presenting that person to the workplace, work takes on a whole new meaning and energy. If you are going to achieve work that you find more fulfilling, it is essential that you begin to get to know yourself. The process that we are working on throughout this book requires you to think of yourself as one person with one life, so in this particular section, we are going to explore your identity and help you to get better acquainted with who you really are and what you really want from your job.

Ch. 6
WILL THE REAL YOU PLEASE STAND UP!

If you want work that is right for you and work that works for you, you have got to know you! 'Work that works for you' is a concept that I have been developing in my own life over the past five years. Put simply, this is work that is aligned with who you really are and what you want to achieve in your life.

The question of 'who are you?' is an age-old question, one that philosophers, psychologists and theologists alike have posed since time began. And whilst it is not my aim to get into a deep debate on the issue, I am suggesting that this is a very worthwhile question that you must begin to ask yourself if you want to do something about being fed up at work.

There has never been a more important time in history to really know who you are and what you are about

We are living in extraordinary times and there is no doubt that the world of work is changing rapidly. There has never been a more important time to know who you are and what you bring to the marketplace table.

The internet and massive leaps forward in technology mean that the consumer or customer has become very powerful. We have unprecedented choice about where we shop and have access to a world wide market at the click of a very portable button. As consumers with this amount of leverage, we can afford to be demanding, so businesses and organisations that are serious about staying afloat in these choppy marketplace waters are forced to become more and more creative about how to engage customer attention and meet our demands.

What has this got to do with you if you are fed up at work? Well, a whole lot; think about it… the businesses and organisations that employ us, (and this applies even if we employ ourselves) have to meet the needs of the demanding consumer through YOU, their staff. So the approach employers take to think about, recruit and manage staff is having to shift to allow them to hold on to existing customers and attract new ones. This shift is already taking place, and even though on a daily basis we are bombarded with news and reports of job cuts and stories of professional posts that have been literally wiped out; the interesting thing is that, increasingly, the work traditionally carried out by professionals in those full time roles are now commissioned to consultants, specialists and contractors recognised for their expertise and quality offering to enhance specific projects. These experts are sought after because of their reputation and personal brand and they move around the market place as customer demands dictate.

I truly believe that we are moving rapidly towards a time when the career, as we know it, will be overtaken by the specialist supplier/producer and that employers will simply not be able to accommodate employees whose performance reflects a lack of enthusiasm and interest for what they are doing on the job. In short we believe that there has simply never been a more crucial time to find and develop a passion for what you do at work. The future of the marketplace is only truly bright for professionals that shine and stand out, and this comes when you're doing what's right for you and what you really love to do.

What we are really talking about here is identity. It is widely agreed that identity formation is a complex and ongoing process that is affected by biology, genetics, environment, relationships, experiences, culture and so on. Identity is a fluid concept which means that there are aspects of it that can be changed, which is good news – particularly if there are things about yourself that you discover are contributing to your negative experience in the workplace. There are however, aspects of your identity that never change. Knowing and acknowledging these crucial facets of your being will serve as fuel to motivate you through the process of change. I call these unchangeable parts of your identity 'core truths' and they apply to all of us, even though we do not always recognise them.

Core truth number one: You have potential

What do I mean by potential? Imagine you are holding a seed in your hand, say a plum seed; it is small, a bit rough around the edges, odd-shaped, doesn't look like much and can easily be mistaken for waste in relation to the juicy flesh of the plum. However, inside this seed is everything that is required for it to become a beautiful plum tree. That plum tree will eventually bear more fruit and in each fruit will be more seed which when planted produces more plum trees and so on. As you examine the seed, the trees have not yet manifested but the possibility for them is real and exists within the seed at that very moment.

Just like the plum seed, we too have hidden possibilities inside and that is your potential. This is true whether you believe it or not, whether you tap into it or not, even whether you like it or not! There is more in us than we can see right now. Myles Munroe, a favourite speaker and author of mine, once said, "The richest place on earth is the graveyard." His point here is that too many of us are buried with this rich possibility locked firmly inside us, never having shared it with the world.

Core truth number two: You are purposed

Keeping with the analogy of the seed, a tree once grown, serves many purposes, the greatest of which is to affect the atmosphere we live in and control the climate by mopping up our carbon dioxide output and providing us with oxygen. The tree also serves to feed people and animals with its fruits, to make furniture, paper and other useful objects for people to use, and to provide shade and shelter. In other words, the tree has the purpose of serving the planet and the people in it in various ways.

Purpose is part of the tree's design – it is the reason the tree exists. In the same way, you are born with purpose. Just like the tree, I want to suggest that your purpose is not so much something you choose, but rather something that you have been designed for. Your purpose is inbuilt – it is what you are born to do; in fact, more than that, it is what you are born to be, it is who you are! Rather than inventing a purpose, we should be embarking on a process of discovery of what our purpose is. It is as we discover and flow in our purpose that life becomes most meaningful, enjoyable and fulfilling.

Core truth number three: You are equipped for impact

Every aspect of the metaphorical tree I have been speaking about has something to do with its purpose and potential. For example, the chemicals within the leaves react with the environment to produce oxygen and the root system draws water from the earth to become rain in an amazing recycling process that helps nourish the earth and control the climate. In the same way, you are a rich blend of characteristics, attributes and experiences that are designed to equip you to make an impact in the world – even some of the things you do not like about yourself have a function that contributes to this purpose!

Of course these three truths are not the only truths about you but acknowledging, exploring and discovering your life purpose, potential and your unique ability to make an impact will give you invaluable information for your bag. Ultimately, pursuing and renewing a lively interest in these aspects of yourself will help you to discern, understand and make decisions about what is really and truly right for you. To help you make a start with this, the next chapter outlines some of life's gifts to you that you may have overlooked or taken for granted, but nevertheless gifts that you must begin to appreciate if you are to move forward in your work life.

Ch. 7
ACKNOWLEDGE YOUR GIFTS

In the last chapter, we identified three core truths about you, which are that you have potential, you are purposed and you are equipped for impact. Even if at this point you do not feel that you have what it takes to achieve a more purpose-driven, meaningful and fulfilling work life, it is important to realise that you have been given a set of 'gifts' to help you along the way.

Essentially, these gifts are the things that we often take for granted but are absolutely vital to living a life of impact. They are those things you did not ask for and have no control over but have been given to you to maximise your ability to make an impact. Take a look at the following list of gifts – everything here is yours for the taking and as you acknowledge them you will be equipping and empowering yourself to make and sustain improvements both in and out of the workplace.

The gift of life

When I work with people who are fed up at work, they often perceive that they do not have what it takes to change their situation. If you can identify with this, it is important to acknowledge that life itself is a gift – the very fact that you are alive is proof that you have something to bring to the table and proof that you have what it takes to change your present circumstances.

The gift of talent and skills

Often people confuse gifts and talents but it is important to recognise that there is a distinction between the two. Talents, though they are gifts, refer to those natural abilities that we are born with; it is the ability to do something well. Skill isn't necessarily naturally acquired but can be learnt and developed to become a talent. Talents and skills can be creative, such as the ability to sing, dance or act, but it can also be something like being really good at maths or being exceptionally good at communicating.

Culturally, there is often a higher value placed on certain talents and skills. The result of this can be that people with less valued traits can mistakenly consider themselves (or be considered) as being without talent or skill – this is not the truth. Every single one of us has talent and skills that equip us to make an impact in our world. In the next section, you will have an opportunity to begin to explore your own skills and talents which will give you more information for the bag.

The gift of your experiences

One of the most common excuses that clients offer when I ask them why they put up with being fed up at work is that they do not have experience to do anything else..I beg to differ – if you are old enough to be fed up at work, you are old enough to have some experience under your belt! In fact, experience is a great teacher and that which is learned through experience rather than abstract reasoning, is often more firmly embedded in your mind and more easily translated to future application and adaptation. The trouble is that people often fail to recognise the value of their professional and personal experience and how it might relate to the marketplace. Even bad experiences that you may wish never happened can have a function and be used to make a significant impact.

Aristotle once said, "For the things we have to learn before we can do them, we learn by doing them". Everything you have experienced has taught you something that can bring value to your ability to make an impact in someone else's life. You may just need to look at your experiences with a fresh pair of eyes and some support to recognise it for what it is.

The gift of your passions, likes and dislikes

We all have things we like and things we dislike which have been shaped by our natural makeup and our experiences so far in life. Most people do not consider these as gifts but I do because our likes and dislikes are drivers of impact as they stimulate us to take action. In fact, they are actually big clues to our purpose as we are most likely to have impact in areas we feel strongly about – whether this is positively or negatively. When we like or dislike something intensely, this generates passion.

71

Some people find it difficult to identify what they are passionate about. Often this is a result of being so fed up and under-stimulated for such a long time that it is easy to believe that you do not have passion or that you do not care enough to like or dislike anything. But even if your passions are lying dormant, they can be revived or stimulated to greatly improve your ability to impact your life and your world.

The gift of other people

Another gift we often do not always acknowledge is the gift of other people. This is not necessarily just the people you know now, but also people who have made an impression on you in the past and people who you will meet in the future that will make a difference in your life. There is no doubt about the fact that we need other people to help us make an impact – a case in point is this book: as I'm writing it, I have impact in mind but the impact would be limited without the expertise of my editor who is helping me to craft and structure the words on this page so that it makes sense to you. She is a gift to me, one that enables me to help you. Now, imagine what would happen if you began to see your employers and managers as gifts to help you make an impact; wouldn't work take on a whole new meaning…?

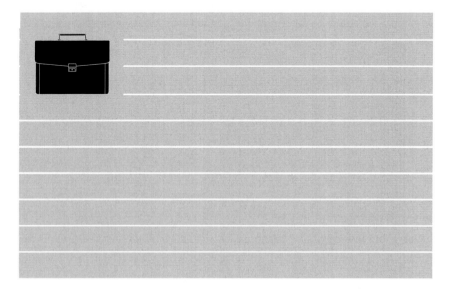

Ch. 8
GATHER THE EVIDENCE

If you have never asked yourself the question "Who am I, really?", you are not alone. It simply has not occurred to some that this is a worthwhile question nor is it always an obvious one to ask when self-awareness is lacking. This is not a question you can ask and answer in one sitting; rather it is a discovery that requires commitment and a relentless curiosity on your part. As I previously mentioned, you must take on the role of a super sleuth – Columbo, my favourite TV detective, solves even the most intricate of mysteries because of his tenacious determination to uncover clues and pursue them until he discovers what they were revealing all along.

Likewise, your individual blend of characteristics, desires and attributes are clues that reveal evidence about who you really are and what your purpose and potential might be. As you uncover these clues, exercise the three levels of why in order to dig deeper and get to the root of who you really are. Coming up are a series of questions to help you do just that.

Please note that the questions in this exercise are not a search for faults, more so, they are what I like to call an "appreciative enquiry". This means that it is really about delving into the full picture of who you are. When you are fed up, it is easy to be over-critical of yourself and to only focus on the negative. Avoid doing that here, but rather be sure to also appreciate the things about yourself that are good. Remember, you are not being marked on your answers; this exercise is purely for your own benefit so do not get hung up on trying to give impressive answers, rather just be true to yourself.

As you come up with answers, examine what you are learning about yourself and see if you can identify the underlying values, beliefs, attitude, skills & capabilities, and behaviour & habits that are behind the things you acknowledge about yourself. If you continually find you do not know the answers, this in itself is information for the bag. Discovering that you do not know yourself perhaps as well as you thought you did is indeed a powerful revelation, one that I hope will steer you into a state of determination to find out more about the undiscovered you. Remember, the reason you are doing this is because you want to create a work life that is right for you and to do this, it requires that you know who you are!

The exercise

Write down your answer to each of the following questions in the space provided:

QUESTION 1: WHAT ARE YOU NATURALLY GOOD AT?

A) What do you like about this?

B) Why is this important to you?

What can you learn about yourself from your answers to B?
(Think about your values, belief, attitude, behaviour and habits)

QUESTION 2: WHAT ACTIVITIES MAKE YOU HAPPY AND GIVE YOU JOY AT HOME?

A) What do you like about this?

B) Why is this important to you?

What can you learn about yourself from your answers to B?
(Think about your values, belief, attitude, behaviour and habits)

QUESTION 3: WHAT ARE YOUR FAVOURITE ASPECTS OF YOUR JOB?

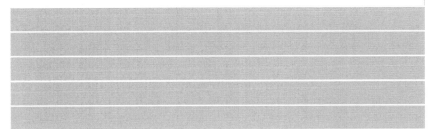

A) What do you like about this?

B) Why is this important to you?

What can you learn about yourself from your answers to B?
(Think about your values, belief, attitude, behaviour and habits)

QUESTION 4: WHAT DO YOU DISLIKE WITH A PASSION?

A) What do you like about this?

B) Why is this important to you?

What can you learn about yourself from your answers to B?
(Think about your values, belief, attitude, behaviour and habits)

QUESTION 5: WHAT JOB WOULD YOU DO EVEN IF YOU WERE NOT BEING PAID TO DO IT?

A) What do you like about this?

B) Why is this important to you?

What can you learn about yourself from your answers to B?
(Think about your values, belief, attitude, behaviour and habits)

QUESTION 6: WHAT REALLY BOTHERS OR WORRIES YOU ABOUT THE WORLD?

A) What do you like about this?

B) Why is this important to you?

What can you learn about yourself from your answers to B?
(Think about your values, belief, attitude, behaviour and habits)

QUESTION 7: WHAT DO OTHER PEOPLE LIKE ABOUT YOU?

A) What do you like about this?

B) Why is this important to you?

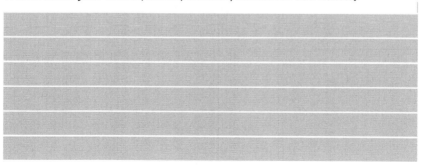

What can you learn about yourself from your answers to B?
(Think about your values, belief, attitude, behaviour and habits)

QUESTION 8: WHO DO YOU GREATLY ADMIRE? (THEY COULD BE ALIVE OR DECEASED)

A) What do you like about them?

B) Why is this important to you?

What can you learn about yourself from your answers to B?
(Think about your values, belief, attitude, behaviour and habits)

QUESTION 9: WHAT DO YOU LIKE THE MOST ABOUT YOUR LIFE?

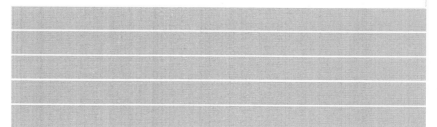

A) What do you like about this?

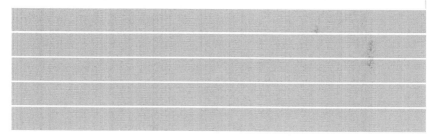

B) Why is this important to you?

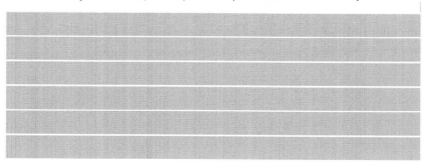

What can you learn about yourself from your answers to B?
(Think about your values, belief, attitude, behaviour and habits)

If you are struggling to identify answers to some or all of these questions or if your answers are only identifying weaknesses but failing to uncover your strengths, I want to reassure you that you do have strengths and it may well be that you need some additional support to uncover them.

It might help if you talk about these questions with a friend or family member who knows you well and who you can trust. It is amazing what can come up as you share and listen to other people's views and opinions about you. Getting someone to discuss it with you can be really beneficial but a word of caution though – be careful to have the final say on the matter as it is what you think about yourself that will ultimately be of most importance here.

It may also be that you will decide to engage the professional services of a coach or consultant who is trained to remain objective while supporting you on your discovery. Later on in the book we will discuss where this additional help could come from, but for now let us explore the concept of who you are a bit further in the next chapter.

Ch. 9
WHAT ARE YOU GOING TO DO WITH YOU?

Now that you have had a chance to have a good think about yourself, it is time to think about what you want to do with your life. At this stage of the journey, your bag should be bulging with information about what you like and dislike, what you are good at and not so good at, what you believe about yourself or don't believe, and so on. Hopefully you will see from all the information you have gathered up until now that the core truths – you are purposed, you have potential and you are equipped for impact – apply to you. You have a lot to offer the world and what you do with who you are is up to you to decide, it's your choice. You must choose how you want to spend, and indeed "invest" your life.

The key to your fulfilment lies in searching out and committing to the manifestation of your heart's desires. In other words, you must begin to really think about and see in your mind's eye the kind of life that gets your heart racing in excitement, the life that you would most like to live. Ironically, it is as you begin to contribute to the world in this way that you in turn become most fulfilled.

Unleash your imagination

Imagination is a gift that helps you create a vision. It is also a skill that must be practiced and developed, but unfortunately it often deteriorates as we become older and "wiser". Children are masters of imagination. When a little girl puts on her princess dress and sips from an empty cup, there is no way you can tell her that she is not actually a princess and she is not drinking the finest tea in the land, because in her imagination that is precisely what is happening and to her it is very real. Because it is real to her, it is not only possible, it is actual. This is the power of imagination – it makes the unreal real.

You see, everything that comes into existence originates in the imagination. Whatever you want to accomplish, you must first build a vision of that thing and commit to seeing it through, rather like starting with the end in mind. Just like an athlete who at the start of the race is already picturing the joy of being first at the finishing line, or an architect painstakingly planning a building or structure that does not yet exist but all the same seeing what the building will look like and how it will function long before the first brick is ever laid, so too must you begin to see the life you want to live in your mind's eye, even though at the moment it may seem so far away or even impossible.

It is time for you to think about what you truly want to do with your life and I have an exercise that will help you to do just that. But before we get to that part, here are some guidelines to bear in mind:

1) Think holistic

Notice here that I am asking you to imagine the life you want rather than the work life you want. We will definitely be looking at your work life later on, but for now it is important to understand that work is just a part of your life and will only improve at a real level as the rest of your life begins to line up with who you really are. Make the picture as full as possible.

2) Avoid the 'shoulds'

This part of the process isn't about what you should want or what you should be doing, rather it requires that you become totally embracing of what is for you. Do not apologise if what you want is not in line with what others think or what circumstances dictate you should be doing with your life – this is not about everybody else for now, it is about you. Avoid the temptation to try pleasing or matching up to anyone else but yourself here.

3) Don't worry about the 'how'

Sometimes people limit what they allow themselves to admit that they want simply because they cannot see how they could possibly make it happen. Knowing 'how' is very rarely a privilege at this point of the process, 'how' reveals itself as you go. Martin Luther King said it this way: "You don't need to see the whole staircase, only the first step." In other words, subsequent steps appear as you take the first step. Admittedly this can feel scary and uncertain but if it were any other way, there would be no need for this book because everyone would be stepping out and making changes in their life!

4) Avoid being "realistic"

You are not doing yourself any favours trying to be 'realistic' at this point. In fact, who decides what is realistic anyway? For the most part, what is realistic to you now is only based on what you know at this present moment. One of my favourite speakers, Les Brown, says that most people are miserable in life not because they aimed too high and missed, but because they aimed too low and hit! Don't let fear or failure rob you of the future you truly desire. Your imagination has the ability to make unrealistic things a possibility so you should not limit yourself by thinking within realistic boundaries, there will be plenty of time for that later on. For now the important thing is to acknowledge your truest desires, no matter how wild and unrealistic they may appear to be.

5) Fuel the passion

As you do this, you should be feeling the excitement, the anticipation and the joy of living the life you are thinking about. We are talking passion here – your deepest desires! If your heart isn't racing and you are not filled with glee as you think and see this imagined future, I need you to ask yourself why. Perhaps you are not dreaming big enough, or perhaps you are still trapped in the 'should' zone. Some need more help than others to break this bad habit and we will come to that later on in the book.

6) Train your imagination

Your imagination is like any muscle in your body – if you fail to use it, it will weaken over a period of time. If you find it a struggle to carry out imagination exercises, it may be because your imagination has not been well used over the years. For some, the difficulty lies in using the imagination for good things because it has become more of a habit to picture your fears, worst-case scenarios and what you don't want. If you find yourself doing this, the first thing to do is put this information in the bag and then make a decision to keep pulling your imagination back in line with your true desires. There is no shortcut to mastering this; just like any habit, it requires that you acknowledge it, make a commitment to change it and then get on with the process.

Okay, so now that we've got the guidelines out of the way, I want you to have a go at the vision exercise below.

The Vision Exercise

Imagine that it is the morning of your 80th birthday: you are sitting at your desk and you are looking back over your life with a smile on your face, everything is as it should be. You are very pleased with what you have accomplished and you have come to the realisation that your life has truly exceeded your own expectations. You decide to write a journal entry about all that you have become, all that you have done and all that you possess.

Using the space below or another sheet of paper, describe what you see as you look back over your life. Remember, in this scene you are not becoming, you are; you are not getting, you have; you are not doing, you have done. Just like the young princess we talked about earlier, I want you to really go there in your mind. Feel the feelings associated with such a satisfying and accomplished life; see yourself whole and complete.

Consider the following:
• What have you achieved with your life?
• Who has benefited from your life and what do they have to say about you?
• How have you invested your skills and talents?
• What is your legacy?

Give yourself some time to do this. You may want to make several drafts and add things as they come to you. Once you have finished, check the following: Does reading this vision excite you? Have you put everything in? Are you sure this is a true reflection of what you want your life to look like?

When you are pleased with the answers, write or type out your final vision. Put as much effort as you can into making it look nice, perhaps framing or laminating it and displaying it somewhere you can see it easily and regularly without too much effort. Your written vision statement is the picture of the end result. Staying with the analogy of the architect, the words on the paper are like the artist's impression of what the building will look like on completion. Now the real work begins…

Ch. 10
IT'S YOURS FOR THE TAKING

If you have completed the exercise in the last chapter, you should now have a vision statement for your life based on what YOU truly desire. So, how are you feeling about it?

Feelings at this point are often mixed. On the one hand you may feel a strong desire and excitement about the picture you have created in your mind's eye for your future; but on the other hand, you may also experience a simultaneous "downer" which, when explored, usually consists of doubt and belief that what you want is never going to happen or that you cannot manage to create all that you have written on paper. People usually say to me, "I just can't see how!" Seeing how is not a prerequisite for success; in fact, if you take a look at anyone who has ever, in your estimation, achieved their biggest truest desires for their lives, they will invariably tell you about the risk they took – stepping out when there seemed to be no path and jumping and learning to fly on the way down! So do not be alarmed that you cannot see how as yet; you simply start by making a decision to have what you want.

Simple but not easy

I've heard time and time again, "Dion, it can't be that simple. I can't just decide that I am going to have this fabulous life." My answer is always the same: it is that simple! However, simple is not the same as easy – if it were easy then everyone would decide to live the life they want. You simply MUST decide to have what you desire. Most people never make this decision and that is the single most important reason why most people never get what they truly want. The world is full of gifted, talented people who have purpose and potential but are fed up at work, fed up at home and fed up with the mediocrity of their life just because they have not decided to do anything about it. Why? I believe it is because we live in a world where people believe that you simply cannot have what you want, that dreams only come true for the very few lucky folks and you should be satisfied with what you are given.

It really matters what you think

So what do you think about this? Do you deserve to have what you imagine? Can you attain it? Do you believe it is possible? These are really important questions to ask and you must search your heart for your truthful answers because it really matters what you think. If you believe that you cannot live the life of your dreams, by just having that belief you will probably prove yourself right. If on the other hand you are able to grab hold of even a glimmer of hope for your future, then that is what it takes to qualify you for the next steps towards it.

The BUT Test!

The BUT test is really a conversation that I want you to have with yourself in order to identify any underlying thoughts and feelings that could jeopardise your ability to develop and achieve your vision. Read over your vision statement again and then finish these statements truthfully:

- I know I should be certain that I can have the life I have dreamed about or something better, BUT......
- I know I should believe that I have what it takes to achieve everything I would like to achieve in life, BUT......
- I know I should feel like I deserve the life I wrote about in my vision statement, BUT......

If you can honestly find no BUTs that is great news, but even if you have a long list of BUTs, that is great information too because these BUTs will consist of fears, doubts, anxieties and limiting thoughts that can potentially hinder your progress and advancement to success. It is not true that you have to be 100% BUT-free to make a start, but you must however acknowledge them and then do what you can to weaken their ability to hold you back. We will deal with this in more detail later on in the book but at this point I want to give you the opportunity to pack some powerful information in the bag that you can use later on to strengthen your resolve and kick your BUTs to the curb!

Kick that BUT!

One way to wage war on the BUTs you have identified is to arm yourself with big strong compelling reasons why you should have the life you have envisioned, and to become familiar with the consequences and what you have to lose if you choose to let the BUTs convince you not to pursue and live it.

Use this space to think about why achieving the life you have envisioned is important, imperative and beneficial to you and other people.

Use this space to think about and list the consequences for you and others if you choose not to go for the life that excites you.

I cannot emphasise enough just how important my own personal list of benefits and consequences have been to me over the years. On difficult days and seasons, they have served as a lifeline and a powerful motivation to keep going when big BUTs threaten to get in the way.

Remember, this is still about making work work for you so if you have found your own list of personal compelling powerful reasons to go on with this process, you are now ready for Section Three.

Section 3
CREATING WORK THAT WORKS FOR YOU

Now that you have had a chance to think about who you really are and what you want your life to be about, the next important part of the process is to work on creating alignment between this and what you do at work. In this section of the book, I want you to look at how your work can fit into your life, and not the other way round, so we are going to really think about the concept of work that works for you – what that means, and how you can begin to create it in your own life.

Ch. 11
PREPARE FOR YOUR VISION

In the last section of the book, we focused on developing a clearer picture of who you really are and what you want to do with your life. So now, it is time to align your work life with this overall vision so that your job becomes an integral part of your strategy for living the life you have envisioned. This is where the real work begins!

Let's face it, if we were able to live that life now we would, but the fact is that there are some things about us that need to be developed and put in place so that we are able to manage and sustain the life we want. In other words, we must get ready for the vision before it arrives. Understanding this is important for a couple of reasons: firstly, because the process of getting ready for what we want and building our expectations for it is like a magnet which somehow attracts exactly what we need to bring us closer to where we want to go. This is commonly referred to as 'the law of attraction'.

The second reason is that just like the old adage, 'if you fail to plan, you plan to fail'. I liken this to lottery winners who spend years dreaming about winning the lottery and becoming a millionaire. When this happens suddenly and the new winners receive what they have longed for, all too often within a short space of time, these instant millionaires find themselves broke and in a much worse position socially than they were before the win. Why does this happen? I believe that in at least some cases, the reason for this is that they were not prepared to handle that type of money. Their inexperience and lack of preparation meant that what should have been a great time in their life became a nightmare.

I doubt very much that when those winners bought their lottery ticket each week for all those years that they thought to themselves, "there's a real risk of me being hurt by a big win". To the contrary, they were probably thinking about the high life and what they were going to spend the money on! It did not seem like there could possibly be a downside, but there was and there is a downside to receiving anything that you are not prepared for. Therefore, in anticipation of living that life you envision, you must begin to prepare yourself and become the kind of person that can manage that type of responsibility.

So this next exercise will begin to raise the awareness in you of what you might need to develop in order to be ready to live the life of your vision and to ensure that you have what it takes to enjoy rather than be hurt by it. I call this the 'Prep List' exercise.

The Prep List exercise

The prep list is about taking a sneak preview into your future to ascertain what it is that you will need to develop now in order to be able to manage and sustain the life that you want in the future. Generally, these attributes and characteristics fall into six categories:

1. Knowledge
2. Experience
3. Character/personality
4. Resources
5. Skills /capabilities
6. Mind-set (values, beliefs etc)

Read through your vision statement again, and on a separate piece of paper, pick out and write a list of all the key features of your vision. For example from your vision statement you may have seen yourself

- A successful entrepreneur
- A big supporter of charities
- Well known or famous in some way
- Making a big difference
- Leading a very happy home

Once you have made your list, take each feature from your vision, one by one, and use the questions below to develop an idea of what you will need to do in order to prepare for, pursue, achieve and sustain the life you have decided you want.

Just like the example above, to fill out the table below, using each of the features that make up your unique vision. By the time you finish completing the table, you should have six lists of attributes that you can begin to to develop in order to create and maintain the life you envision. You may not yet know everything at this stage but that is okay – as you progress, there are ways for you to become more aware of what your vision will require of you. This is all extremely valuable information for the bag, and in particular it will form the foundation of your assessment about what work will work for you.

(Example) In my vision I see myself as...

A successful entrepreneur	
What knowledge do I need to achieve, sustain and enjoy this?	**What Experience do I need to achieve, sustain and enjoy this?**
Setting up a business & Get customers	Being the boss, Managing conflict
Masters in Business	Working under pressure
What Character or personality do I need to achieve, sustain & enjoy this?	**What Resources do I need to achieve, sustain and enjoy this?**
Driven, Confident	Mentor
Determined	Start up Money
What Skills & Capabilities do I need to achieve, sustain and enjoy this?	**What beliefs and mindset do I need to achieve, sustain and enjoy this?**
Project Management,	I can attitude
People leader, Problem solving	

In my vision I see myself as...

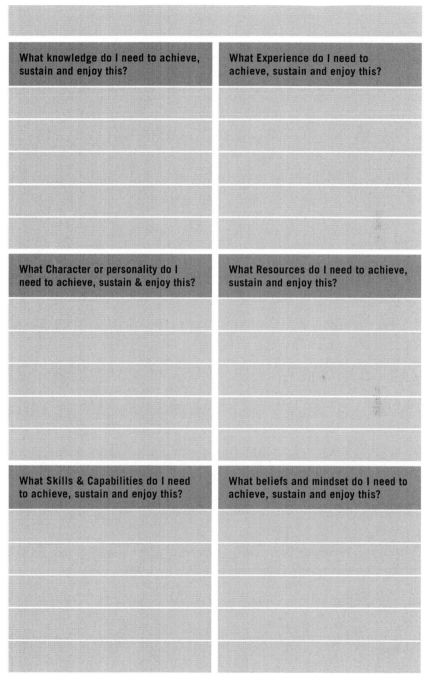

What knowledge do I need to achieve, sustain and enjoy this?

What Experience do I need to achieve, sustain and enjoy this?

What Character or personality do I need to achieve, sustain & enjoy this?

What Resources do I need to achieve, sustain and enjoy this?

What Skills & Capabilities do I need to achieve, sustain and enjoy this?

What beliefs and mindset do I need to achieve, sustain and enjoy this?

In my vision I see myself as...

What knowledge do I need to achieve, sustain and enjoy this?

What Experience do I need to achieve, sustain and enjoy this?

What Character or personality do I need to achieve, sustain & enjoy this?

What Resources do I need to achieve, sustain and enjoy this?

What Skills & Capabilities do I need to achieve, sustain and enjoy this?

What beliefs and mindset do I need to achieve, sustain and enjoy this?

In my vision I see myself as...

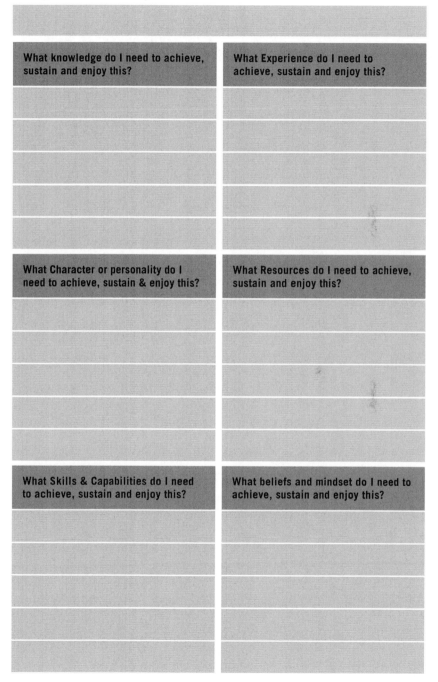

What knowledge do I need to achieve, sustain and enjoy this?

What Experience do I need to achieve, sustain and enjoy this?

What Character or personality do I need to achieve, sustain & enjoy this?

What Resources do I need to achieve, sustain and enjoy this?

What Skills & Capabilities do I need to achieve, sustain and enjoy this?

What beliefs and mindset do I need to achieve, sustain and enjoy this?

In my vision I see myself as...

What knowledge do I need to achieve, sustain and enjoy this?

What Experience do I need to achieve, sustain and enjoy this?

What Character or personality do I need to achieve, sustain & enjoy this?

What Resources do I need to achieve, sustain and enjoy this?

What Skills & Capabilities do I need to achieve, sustain and enjoy this?

What beliefs and mindset do I need to achieve, sustain and enjoy this?

In my vision I see myself as...

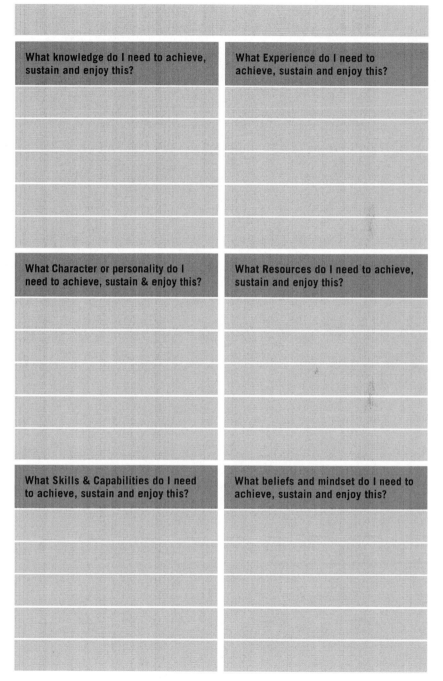

What knowledge do I need to achieve, sustain and enjoy this?

What Experience do I need to achieve, sustain and enjoy this?

What Character or personality do I need to achieve, sustain & enjoy this?

What Resources do I need to achieve, sustain and enjoy this?

What Skills & Capabilities do I need to achieve, sustain and enjoy this?

What beliefs and mindset do I need to achieve, sustain and enjoy this?

In my vision I see myself as...

What knowledge do I need to achieve, sustain and enjoy this?	What Experience do I need to achieve, sustain and enjoy this?

What Character or personality do I need to achieve, sustain & enjoy this?	What Resources do I need to achieve, sustain and enjoy this?

What Skills & Capabilities do I need to achieve, sustain and enjoy this?	What beliefs and mindset do I need to achieve, sustain and enjoy this?

In my vision I see myself as...

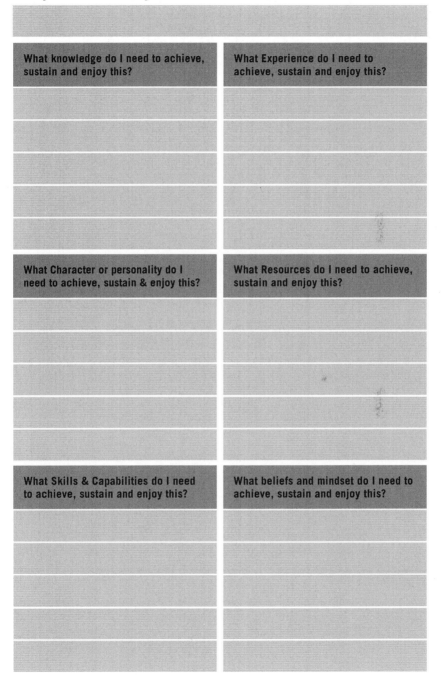

What knowledge do I need to achieve, sustain and enjoy this?

What Experience do I need to achieve, sustain and enjoy this?

What Character or personality do I need to achieve, sustain & enjoy this?

What Resources do I need to achieve, sustain and enjoy this?

What Skills & Capabilities do I need to achieve, sustain and enjoy this?

What beliefs and mindset do I need to achieve, sustain and enjoy this?

In my vision I see myself as...

What knowledge do I need to achieve, sustain and enjoy this?	What Experience do I need to achieve, sustain and enjoy this?

What Character or personality do I need to achieve, sustain & enjoy this?	What Resources do I need to achieve, sustain and enjoy this?

What Skills & Capabilities do I need to achieve, sustain and enjoy this?	What beliefs and mindset do I need to achieve, sustain and enjoy this?

In my vision I see myself as...

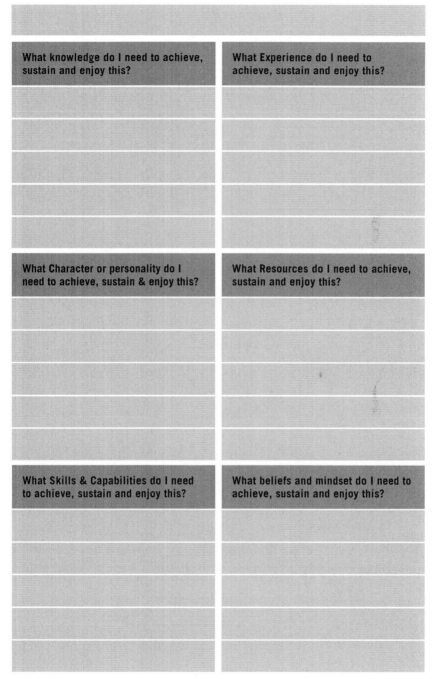

What knowledge do I need to achieve, sustain and enjoy this?

What Experience do I need to achieve, sustain and enjoy this?

What Character or personality do I need to achieve, sustain & enjoy this?

What Resources do I need to achieve, sustain and enjoy this?

What Skills & Capabilities do I need to achieve, sustain and enjoy this?

What beliefs and mindset do I need to achieve, sustain and enjoy this?

Ch. 12
FINDING THE RIGHT JOB FOR YOU

The sad fact is that not everyone that is fed up at work is serious about doing something about it. If you have come this far in the book, I think it is safe to assume that you are not in this category and you are serious about engaging in work that is right for you. To help you with this, my aim in this chapter is to make suggestions about the characteristics that make a job right for you. However, you must remember that one size does not fit all in the world of work so use the information in your bag so far to determine what 'right' means for you where work is concerned.

The following are five key characteristics of a job that is right for you:

A right job...relates to your vision and aspirations

This is perhaps one of the points I want to make most strongly in this book because I believe it is the key to finding fulfilment at work and in life.

I recently met a young man, 24 years old, who shared with me his dream to be a football coach for his favourite football team. The first thing I noticed as he spoke was that I did not see the sparkle in his eyes or hear that tell-tale tone in his voice that I usually hear when someone is sharing from their heart. What was even more noticeable was that as an office manager for the company I was meeting with, his current job was unrelated, in his thinking, to his dream of being a football coach. When I asked him about this, he said, "I am just doing this job in the meantime."

It transpired that not only was his job not remotely connected to his dream, his lifestyle was not lined up either. He does not play football, he was not particularly fit and he was not consciously developing any of the skills that would be required of him as a premiership coach. I could not help but wonder what the chances of him achieving his "dream" was or if indeed it really was his dream!

In short, work that is right for you should be much more than just being able to do the job or simply collecting a decent pay packet at the end of the month. I am suggesting that you align your work with your life purpose and aspirations and with what you are to accomplish – ultimately, a job is right for you when it is offering you the opportunity to experience or become equipped to experience that which is important in your life.

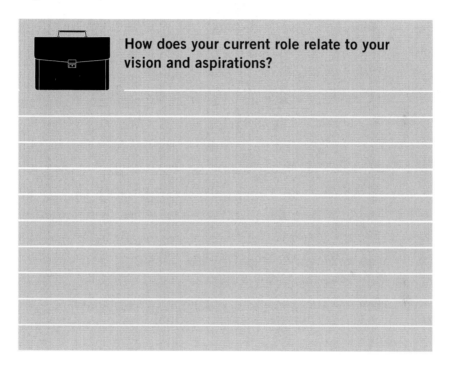

How does your current role relate to your vision and aspirations?

A right job...draws on your strengths, skills and talents

This might seem obvious but it is important to note, nonetheless. A job that is right for you will offer you an opportunity to play to your biggest strengths and abilities. Operating in your natural and acquired talents will increase and improve your experience of work and give you an opportunity to keep these attributes fresh and sharp. High level skill and talent naturally translates to high level performance, therefore a job that draws on your strongest talents will have a direct impact on your level of performance at work – I have yet to meet anyone who does not like the thrill of a job well done!

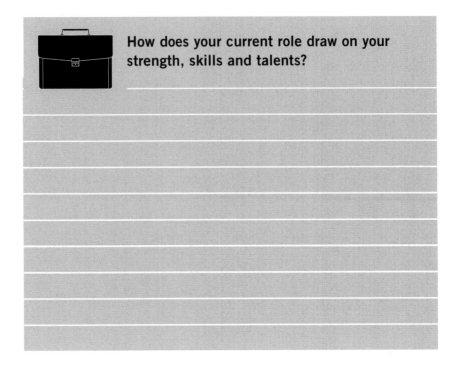

How does your current role draw on your strength, skills and talents?

A right job... connects with your passions

A job that is right for you will provide you with an opportunity to come into regular contact with and have an impact on whatever it is you care about or feel strongly about. If your passion is related to hunger in developing countries, domestic violence or maybe global warming, a job that is right for you will grant you opportunities to be in close contact with the issue and/or in some way impact it. This reminds me of a friend of mine who works for the church. He is a Bishop but he is also an author, a motivational speaker, internet marketer and a business coach. These roles may seem diverse at first glance but they are not at all because each of them allow him to connect with his overall passion for global financial freedom and independence.

Similarly, I am a midwife, an author, a business consultant and a Work engagement specialist and each role is directly related to my passion for equipping people to conceive, develop and birth what they are "carrying" – whether that is a vision or a real baby! Effectively, that is my motive for writing this book. Ultimately, passion is the fuel that makes the job easy, even on days when it gets hard. It is the force that keeps you engaged and loving what you do when all else fails.

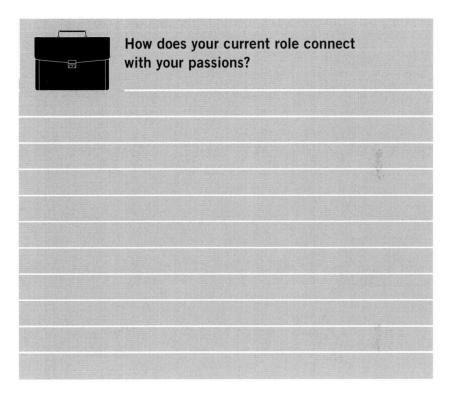

How does your current role connect with your passions?

A right job... challenges your weaknesses

A job that pulls on areas in which you lack strength can be of huge benefit to you. This is a largely overlooked, but very important, criteria for the right job. At first thought it may not seem to make sense that a job that highlights and challenges your weaknesses, deficits and incompetence is beneficial; in fact, many people will avoid roles that will potentially require them to use an attribute that they are not particularly strong in. However, such a job can offer great opportunity for you to grow and develop new skills and capacity that will serve you well in your future.

Recently a client of mine discovered that in order to take the next steps towards the life of her vision, she would need to communicate with and write several reports to a high-level government department. She was experiencing a severe bout of procrastination in taking this step and on exploration, we identified that it was because she was uncomfortable with that level of meeting and communication. On reflection though, she was able to recognise that in a previous role years before, she worked for 18 months in a department very much like the one she would need to contact now, but she confessed to having always avoided the parts of the role that would have given her exactly the experience she would be pulling on right now. Perhaps if she had envisaged that she would need the experience years later she would have used the 18 months to deliberately expose herself to challenges that would help to develop her in these areas.

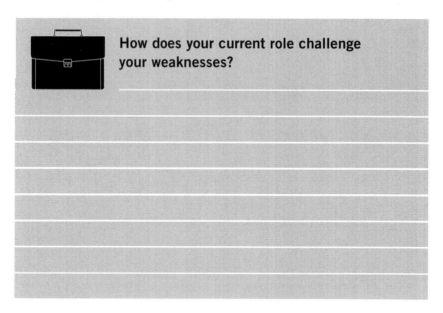

How does your current role challenge your weaknesses?

A right job... increases your value to others

If you consider that your value to other people in and out of the marketplace is based upon the level of problem you can solve or the level to which you can meet a need, then a job that is right for you will be equipping you with the relevant knowledge, experience and networks that will increase your ability to solve problems and challenges and to meet needs in order to have the impact you want to have in your world. You should be assessing what the organisation or company has to offer you in terms of new and up to date learning that will support your commitment to your vision and aspirations.

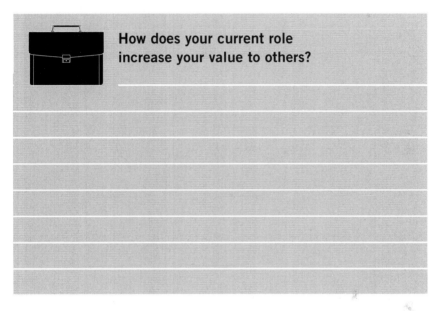

How does your current role increase your value to others?

Now that you have identified some characteristics of a right job, it is time to decide whether or not your current job is right for you. The next chapter will better help you with this decision...

Ch. 13
SHOULD I STAY OR SHOULD I GO? IT'S DECISION TIME!

The exercise in the last chapter was designed to help you to take a frank look at whether or not your current job is right for you. The question, 'should I stay or should I go?' is a crucial question because what you do about changing the fact that you are fed up at work depends on how you answer it.

Admitting that your job is wrong for you can be scary because it forces you to make decisions about whether or not you are going to do something about it. Equally, admitting that a job is right for you when you have already made up your mind to quit and jump ship for whatever reason (perhaps someone or something at work is making things difficult for you), can also be scary because in deciding to do the right thing and stay, you then have to face up to the people or circumstances that you are running away from. Both scenarios can be seriously daunting and it may not even be too clear in your mind at this point which is the lesser of the two evils – should I stay or should I go?

It's decision time!

Of course the decision is one that only you can and should make, after all, this is your life we are talking about and you are the expert. There are many things to consider here: For example, at the time of writing this, the media is dominated with headlines about the gloomy economic climate and on a daily basis we hear news of soaring unemployment rates and redundancies. People are genuinely afraid to rock the proverbial job market boat right now. There seems to be a subliminal message in the air that the chances of getting a job are dire therefore any job is better than no job at all.

Apart from the current economic crisis, there are other personal stories and circumstances that might complicate the decision about whether or not you should stay in your current job. Recently, I was having a conversation with a client who was explaining that he had been fed up for about 18 months and was really disliking going to work. Initially he had only taken the position for three months but eighteen months later he was still there. He explained that he was making the decision to "put up with it" because he needed to raise money for his fast-approaching wedding. Of course this is understandable, however, be aware that it is likely that you will almost invariably be able to find a reason, or dare I say an excuse, to stay just because leaving seems too much like hard work and before you know it, you may find yourself becoming stuck in a very deep rut.

A quick word about decision-making

'Decision' is a common term, one that is used a lot and rolls off the tongue with relative ease. But the fact is that not everything we call a decision is actually a decision. What we often mean is that we would like a particular outcome so we are prepared to "give it a go," or "see how it goes". This approach to decision-making is usually loaded with an unconscious escape clause that implies that if it gets too hard or challenging, then we will just give up.

However, the word decision comes from the latin word 'decisio' which means 'to cut off'. At its root, the word decision is related to the term 'covenant' or 'solemn agreement'. This implies that making a decision is far from a frivolous flippant wish, rather, it is about making an agreement with yourself to cut off any other possibility than that which you are pursuing. It involves commitment and implies a willingness to be tenacious in your pursuit of the thing, whatever that may be.

To make a true decision is to completely acknowledge and embrace the fact that you are likely to encounter adversity, challenges, hardships and disappointments along the way, but yet still resolve in your heart that despite whatever comes your way, you will continue to pursue your vision and make it happen.

Here is my only advice in support of you making what I recognise can be a tough decision:

1) Stay or go because it is the right thing to do

It is important that you be completely honest with yourself and make a decision to do the right thing for you, even if it is daunting. Be objective about weighing up the pros and cons of both scenarios and keep your commitment to the life you have envisioned at the forefront of your thinking to keep yourself on the right track.

2) Stay or go because you choose to

If for whatever reason you would prefer to stay in a job that you are fed up with rather than face the process of finding the right job for you or facing the person or situation that is interfering with your fulfillment at work, that is completely your choice. Many people choose to stay where they are ultimately because their values and beliefs tell them that where they are right now is better than taking up the perceived risk and challenge of moving. There is no law against being fed up at work so if you recognise yourself here you do not have to make excuses or answer to anyone, you can simply own your decision. What I recommend however is that you keep this book and continue to add information to your bag until the time you are ready to take things further.

If you have made the decision to do something about being fed up at work, then you are ready to move on to the final section of the book where we will begin to look ahead and prepare for the reality of the journey in front of you.

But first, I want you to make a real decision and commitment to making things better at work for you. Take a look at the statement of intention below. Read it through and sign it if you agree with what it says. Signing this statement sends a message to your subconscious mind that this is something serious and important for your life.

As a further demonstration of your commitment, please go to my website **www.fed upatwork.com** and sign up online to tell us that you have made this commitment. It is free and easy and we will email you a certificate to memorialise this critical step that you have just taken.

Statement of intention

In view of what I have learnt so far, I now understand that work offers an important opportunity to express my true self and to develop and equip me for all that I will achieve in my life.

I have written down what I can see in my future and I commit to taking responsibility for making it (or something better) happen. I hereby promise that I will actively pursue work that enables change and growth in my character, skills, experience, resources and knowledge so that my vision becomes a reality.

I realise that the process may be difficult and challenging at times but I know that I have what it takes to succeed despite any obstacles that may stand in my way.

Signed	
Date	
Printed Name	
Witnessed by	
Dated	
Printed Name	

Section 4
PREPARE FOR THE JOURNEY AHEAD

Well done for getting to this point in the book, I hope you are feeling ready and raring to go with your new life at work! By now your bag should be packed with lots of information, ideas, aspirations and tools that are unique to you and that will serve you well as you move forward. I'm going to be honest with you: the weeks and months ahead are likely to be challenging as you begin to actively pursue change, so this next section is designed to strengthen, prepare and empower you for the journey ahead.

Ch. 14
EMBRACE RESPONSIBILITY FOR YOUR LIFE

It was Winston Churchill that said "the best ability is availability" and whilst I agree that availability is important, it is my view that the best ability is 'responsibility'. Taking responsibility for your life is perhaps the most important thing you can do if you are serious about making changes. It requires that you begin to see yourself as the only person with whom the buck stops as far as your life is concerned.

To accept responsibility for where you are at work and for where you want to go requires you to say that "everything that has happened to me up until this point has happened because I allowed it to; where I am, I am here because I brought myself to this place." Not everyone is prepared to accept responsibility to this extent. Accepting responsibility is all about ownership of your life and what happens in it; it stems from a premise that you have the authority to determine your response to whatever you come into contact with.

The problem with blame

Taking responsibility is risky because you take away the sometimes comfortable option of blaming other people and circumstances for where you are, because blame is the alternative to taking responsibility.

Everyday, I come into contact with people who tell me that they are fed up at work but they are not the problem. They describe things, people and circumstances in their jobs that make their work lives difficult, pointing out that they have no control over these and therefore no control over the effects they have on their lives. It is true that 'stuff' happens; it is also true that life sometimes throws mighty challenges at you that either knock you for six or make progress very difficult.

The other day I was watching a political debate on TV where the panel were answering questions on the impact of the credit crunch. One lady got up to make her point: she was shouting at the panel with rage, demanding to know what they were going to do about her personal financial situation which she put down to the credit crunch. After a long rant, she said something that hit me like a ton of bricks, she said,

"I find myself in this situation through no fault of my own!" She had completely absolved herself of all responsibility for her situation and now she was looking for someone else, in this case the government, to blame and to also sort it out.

When we get into the place where we feel helpless, it is easy to point the finger and often it is blame that helps us cope with our situation and circumstance. I call blame a robber because it robs us of the ability and responsibility to make the changes we need to make. We live in a blame culture and the reason that it is difficult to take responsibility is that you open yourself up to being seen to make a mistake and this is uncomfortable for many people. It is really important to recognise and understand that this journey to making work work for you can only happen as you accept responsibility.

You are going to really need to take responsibility because the road ahead is likely to have barriers, hindrances and obstacles that will threaten to make the journey difficult. Taking responsibility is the prerequisite to overcoming these, as you will see in the next chapter.

Ch. 15
DEALING WITH PROCESS AND BARRIERS

Process is really important. Today we live in a world where we want things when we want them and we want them now! We are the ultimate impatient generation and though there is nothing wrong with the fast pace of today (many things have improved because of it), it often means that we undervalue the importance of process.

Now that you have made a commitment to improve things rather than just covering over your grim state at work, it is important to understand that this cannot happen overnight. Just like any change that is significant and worthwhile, there will be a process involved during which you will encounter challenges, problems, setbacks and barriers.

In this context, we are talking about your work life and indeed the life that you have envisioned for yourself. If your vision is big enough, chances are that you are not ready for it right now and your unique process will be one that ensures that when you arrive at your destination, you have what it takes to maintain, sustain and enjoy it. That is the purpose of process – it is the price that is paid for a quality result. Although you may want to radically transform your work life quickly and easily, the truth of the matter is that the work that will be required to undo those set thoughts, behaviours, habits and beliefs that have brought you to the place of being fed up, will take time and process.

Often, what is difficult about process are the barriers and obstacles that we encounter along the way. I used to believe that some people had it easy in life; that everything was smooth and they did not encounter any problems, but the more I hear and read other people's stories, the more I understand that absolutely nobody is exempt from process and barriers. Barriers are, in my opinion, misunderstood, and many interpret their presence to be an indication that they are disqualified or unable to achieve the desired outcome and as a result they either fail to make progress or worse still, they quit.

Barriers come in all shapes and sizes and relate to anything that prevents progress towards your vision, aspiration or goals. They can be physical, mental, emotional, circumstantial, actual or even imagined. They have a purpose in that they are an essential part of your process. In fact, the process of dealing with barriers is beneficial in itself for many reasons. They are an equipping mechanism that life supplies to you in preparation for where you are going. Just like a workout in the gym, dealing with barriers helps you to create "muscle power" that will ensure you will be able to carry the weight of responsibility that comes with experiencing your vision.

Contrary to popular belief, it is not a bad thing to face barriers, it is actually an opportunity to learn and grow. I like to think of barriers as tests which demand questions of you: How badly do you really want this thing? How much are you prepared to keep going to get it? How big a price are you prepared to pay…? Passing the test requires that you develop a dogged determination to win and an outright refusal to relinquish your desire, and in passing, you become more qualified.

It can seem that the decision to pursue a significant change or outcome at work almost activates the occurrence of barriers. As soon as you lift your foot to move towards your goal, a barrier suddenly presents itself! Barriers and obstacles however have the power to teach you what you did not even know you needed to know. They are catalysts that cause ingenious lessons about life and the power that is in you, allowing you to discover hidden skills and talent.

A man that is determined to overcome barriers because he wants to get to a certain place is a mighty creative force. The presence of the barrier is an agitator to such a man and he simply must find a way to get around, over, across, under or past it! Creativity is often high at this point.

One thing to watch out for are barriers in disguise. Remember that a barrier is anything that is going to stop you from moving forward so it is important to know that even pleasant things might serve this purpose. For example, as great as an unexpected pay rise might be, it may well be the 'barrier' that has the power to stop you from pursuing your vision.

The good thing about barriers is that they can be overcome and this is something that you have to decide to keep in your mind as you embark on this journey. Overcoming barriers and obstacles build character: the more you overcome on the journey towards your vision, the more you realise that you can! It develops a confidence in you that is unshakeable which is a true characteristic of one who lives a fulfilling and worthwhile life of significant impact.

When you begin to grapple with barriers instead of running away from them, it does wonders for your character. Things begin to grow in you – determination grows and equally importantly, your resilience grows.

Ch. 16
BUILDING
RESILIENCE

"The secret of success is to work harder on yourself than you do on your job" **Jim Rohn**

In the earlier chapters, I pointed out that some people, even though they are in the job that is right for them, are still unfulfilled and fed up at work. Whether you go to a new job or you stay in the job that you are in, once you get into the place that is right for you, you may still experience uncomfortable or unpleasant circumstances that make you question whether you are in the right place.

Resilience is the ability to deal with or recover quickly from challenging circumstances or unexpected difficulties at work. Your boss may be a tyrant or your workload demanding, but if you are to get what you want from being in this job, it requires that you find ways to ensure that you stay on track and not get put off the pursuit of your desired outcomes. To put it bluntly, you must develop broad shoulders and a strong back!

Building resilience enables you to remain deliberate about getting what you want from your job, regardless of any circumstance or difficulty. The resilient worker has the ability to remain consistent, on track and determined in the face of adversity and this is what you must be striving for now.

Steps to develop resilience

1) Be clear about you what you want

All the questions and exercises in this book have been asked in order to generate answers or information that will inform your discovery of who you really are and what you really want. If you are to become more resilient, it is crucial that you are clear about what you are aiming to achieve and how where you are now feeds into this. You must choose to develop ways that keep you moving towards your vision, work objectives and goals, rather than away from difficulties.

2) Identify an effective support structure

This will be made up of people you can trust and that you know have your best interests at heart. Preferably you will have allies both in and out of the workplace who are skilled to help you work through the challenges and solve the problems you face, rather than getting distracted and held back by them.

3) Skill up!

Things that challenge your fulfillment and cause you to be fed up at work often spring from relationship and communication issues, therefore in order to increase resilience, it makes good sense to develop your skills in these areas and increase your capacity to communicate and relate effectively, especially during times of conflict.

4) Talk to yourself

When I was growing up people used to say that talking to yourself is the first sign of madness. Later on, I heard others say that talking to yourself is alright but answering yourself back is a sure sign that you are as nutty as a fruit cake! I don't agree with either of these suggestions; I believe that throughout the process of changing your experience at work, you must become your own biggest counsellor, encourager and coach – that means that you talk to yourself! Tell yourself you can make it; remind yourself to keep a long-term perspective, and consider the challenge you face in the broader context. Keep your hope and determination alive and expect good things from life.

5) Learn to manage strong feelings and impulses

The process of change will sometimes strongly make you feel like walking away or acting on an emotional impulse. You will come across people and situations that really press your buttons. Learning to manage your emotions and reactions in difficult times will ultimately make you more resilient. One way to do this is to learn to recognise your triggers and develop coping strategies and techniques that you can employ in times of need.

Ultimately, resilience is a state of mind, body and spirit that will keep you going when the going gets tough. The key to building resilience is self-development, therefore your commitment to working on your Primary Experience Regulators is crucial in this process.

Ch. 17

FINAL TIPS FOR THE ROAD

(Tips for the journey)

Ok so that's it! I hope that you can now see how you became fed up at work in the first place and that you have made a true commitment to make sure you never tolerate being that way again. The process described in this book is the process that is going to transform your work life into one that is meaningful, fulfilling, directed and purposeful. In summary, that process is as follows:

1. Discover the true you and get to know yourself
2. Discover what you want to do with your life
Then...
3. Choose work that will express and develop the true you
4. Commit to and take responsibility for developing your PERs

It is that simple, but as we discussed earlier, simple does not always mean easy. Discovering and staying in tune with who you really are in and out of the workplace can create all sorts of internal and external conflicts, battles and challenges. I do not promise that the transformation journey will always be easy but I do believe that you are capable of staying the course and making it to your desired destination. So here are some final tips to keep you on track as you journey towards not only work that works for you, but a life that works for you.

Keep your bag with you

As you have gone along with this process, you will have been packing your 'bag' with ideas, insights and discoveries about yourself and the life you want to live. Your vision statement is in the bag and your statement of intention is there too. The content of your bag is going to come in handy for your journey forward so keep it with you and have a rummage through on a regular basis to remind yourself of what is in there. Read through your notes and statements regularly and take time to pack any new development, ideas and discoveries that you acquire along the way. This will not only help you to stay on the right track, it is also a fabulous way for you to keep track of where you started, the distance you have travelled and the progress you have made.

Start now

Whether you have decided to stay or leave your current position, I want you to decide to start making the change right now, right where you are – choose to no longer be fed up. Recognise that simply by making the decision to do something about your situation at work means that the journey has already started; you are already on your way and you should have an exciting compelling destination in mind, so act like it! Lift your head up, throw your shoulders back and tell yourself that better days are coming because they are!

Write down three (or more if you want to) goals that you will achieve in the next three months that will move you closer to work that works for you.

For each goal, decide on an action/actions that you can take…
- …today
- …this week
- …this month

Get help

I can tell you from both personal and professional experience that creating change in work and in life will almost certainly provoke a wide range of emotions and responses along the way – from fear and doubt to confusion and feelings of inadequacy. There will be high points and some low points too which is why it is important to identify a support network of people who you will share your plans with and who you know will be there for you to encourage, advise and on the rare meltdown moment, help you to pull things together again.

A word of caution though, choose carefully who you rally up to be on your team because not everyone will understand your decision to move on and grow and the cold hard truth is that even people that love and care about you may have a difficult time listening to what sounds like you harping on about finding yourself, being the real you and aligning your work life with your life purpose!

Of course, I hope that you will also subscribe to my membership site **www.dionjohnson.com** where you will always find inspiration, links to professional services, tools, resources, events information and testimonials to help you on your journey.

The important thing is to surround yourself with people and information that will keep your passion and vision alive.

Conclusion

This book is designed to help you decide to have work that fits with who you are and not a you that fits with the work. Work that works for you is not only your right, it is your obligation because the cost of putting up with being fed up at work is, in my opinion and I hope yours too, a tragic waste of life. I believe that if you invest the time and energy in this process, you will open yourself up to the opportunity that exists to not only express who you really are in the marketplace, but to develop your ability to achieve and sustain the life you envision.

There is a common misconception that generally people do not get what they want in life and that success is the privilege of a very elite few; I beg to differ. You can have work that works for you and it does not have to be an onerous process. Like my daughter once said, "Mummy don't tell people you go to work, tell them you go to play!" Imagine work that you enjoy so much that you call it play! This reminds me of something James Michener said:

"The master in the art of living makes little distinction between his work and his play, his labour and his leisure, his mind and his body, his information and his recreation, his love and his religion. He hardly knows which is which; he simply pursues his vision of excellence at whatever he does, leaving others to decide if he is working or playing. To him he is always doing both."

Ultimately your work life should be taking you somewhere – somewhere of your own choosing and somewhere that is a true reflection of your innermost self. I hope you have discovered that change is indeed possible and that your experience at work is literally what you make it, so if you want it to change for the better you have to be committed to developing yourself. The destination is important but please do not forget to enjoy the journey too!

About the author

Dion Johnson is a dynamic personality with a very successful 20 year career history in Health and Social Care where she established the reputation of trailblazer and leader developing new dynamic services for vulnerable client groups.

Dion is quite simply a master communicator and everything about her life is driven by her desire and passion to Empower, Equip and Encourage everyone she connects with to discover and live bigger more meaningful lives. To this end Dion is an avid and dedicated lifelong learner with interests in theology, sociology and Positive Psychology. Dion is also a Business Practitioner and Master of Neuro Linguistic Programming (NLP) trained by the internationally acclaimed Sue Knight. Dion's superior communication ability is enhanced by her experience as an over comer. She was born with a facial disfigurement that contributed to patterns of poor self esteem and rejection. Her journey is fascinating and is the powerful motivation and foundation on which she is building businesses that will reach individuals and organizations that are experiencing inadequate performance and progress. Her message is one that inspires hope, empowerment and a solution focused zeal for authentic success. Her mantra is "I will practice what I preach"

Dion, now one of the UK's leading Work Engagement Specialists, is an award winning Mentor and Messenger to Managerial Women around the globe and a recognised expert in Work Life Improvement; Employee Engagement: and Feminine Self Leadership. She is the founder of dionjohnson.com and through this company she is reaching the workforce and stirring up a hunger for authentic success in the belly of today's professionals and the organizations that employ them. Dion Lives in South London with her daughter Bianca and 92 years young Grandma Hazel!

To find out more about how Dion can help you or
your organization, log on to her websites now:
dionjohnson.com

Next Step...

Lets Get Better Connected

1. Visit www.DionJohnson.com

2. Put your name and email address in the box provided

3. And we'll get your FREE Get Started Pack winging it's way to you in an instant, with news, updates and powerful insights to assistance you with taking things further!

Join Us Today; I Can't Wait To Meet You...
Here's to your spectacular work life transformation!

"I was dying off, unthinking, unsatisfied, unfulfilled... just trying to make it through the every work day, getting more and more depressed. Working with Dion gave me three profound gifts... hindsight, insight and foresight. I saw my life with fresh eyes and now for the first time in years I'm alive and excited about Monday to Friday!"

Jennie Hargreaves, Sales Executive

Dion J